Long-Term Counselling

PROFESSIONAL SKILLS FOR COUNSELLORS

The *Professional Skills for Counsellors* series, edited by Colin Feltham, covers the practical, technical and professional skills and knowledge which trainee and practising counsellors need to improve their competence in key areas of therapeutic practice.

Titles in the series include:

Medical and Psychiatric Issues for Counsellors
Brian Daines, Linda Gask and Tim Usherwood

Personal and Professional Development for Counsellors
Paul Wilkins

Counselling by Telephone
Maxine Rosenfield

Time-Limited Counselling
Colin Feltham

Client Assessment
Stephen Palmer and Gladeana McMahon (eds)

Counselling, Psychotherapy and the Law
Peter Jenkins

Contracts in Counselling
Charlotte Sills (ed.)

Counselling Difficult Clients
Kingsley Norton and Gill McGauley

Long-Term Counselling

Geraldine Shipton
and Eileen Smith

SAGE Publications
London • Thousand Oaks • New Delhi

First published 1998

SAGE Publications Ltd
6 Bonhill Street
London EC2A 4PU

SAGE Publications Inc.
2455 Teller Road
Thousand Oaks, California 91320

SAGE Publications India Pvt Ltd
32, M-Block Market
Greater Kailash – I
New Delhi 110 048

British Library Cataloguing in Publication data

A catalogue record for this book is available
from the British Library

ISBN 0 7619 5029 X
ISBN 0 7619 5030 3 (pbk)

Library of Congress catalog card number 97–062228

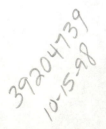

Typeset by Mayhew Typesetting, Rhayader, Powys
Printed in Great Britain by Biddles Ltd, Guildford, Surrey

Contents

Acknowledgements

We should like to thank the many people who helped directly or indirectly with the writing of this book. Particular thanks are due to Colin Feltham for his patient and thoughtful editing. John Morton-Smith kindly read some chapters in draft and commented on them from a person-centred perspective; Penny Spearman read the text and commented from her extensive experience of long-term counselling and her current work on its evaluation. Nicola Barden, Elsa Bell, Julia Buckroyd, Coral Devereau, Bev Harden, Mary McCaffrey, John Rowan, Alan Naylor-Smith, Dorothy Oglesby, Lesley Parker, Libby Wattis, Robert Young and others mentioned by name in the text all engaged in written, electronic or face-to-face discussion of particular points.

Eileen Smith is grateful to the University of Hertfordshire for a term's sabbatical leave to concentrate on writing. Geraldine Shipton wishes to thank Tim Kendall for the use of resources at the Centre for Psychotherapeutic Studies at the University of Sheffield.

List of acronyms

AGCPLB	Advice, Guidance, Counselling and Psychotherapy Lead Body
ASC	Association for Student Counselling (now Association for University and College Counselling)
BAC	British Association for Counselling
BCP	British Confederation of Psychotherapists
BPS	British Psychological Society
COSCA	Confederation of Scottish Counselling Agencies
NVQ	National Vocational Qualifications
UKCP	United Kingdom Council for Psychotherapy

Come what come may,
Time and the hour runs through the roughest day.
(Macbeth, Act 1, Scene 3)

If we had a keen vision and feeling of all ordinary human life, it would be like hearing the grass grow and the squirrel's heart beat, and we should die of that roar that lies on the other side of silence. As it is, the quickest of us walk about well wadded with stupidity.
(George Eliot, Middlemarch, 1965: 226)

1

Introduction

A book on long-term counselling may seem like a contradiction in terms. Many assume that counselling is by its nature short-term only; their associations are to crisis intervention, focus on a single issue, support, discharge of feeling, problem solving or perhaps advice. All of these activities can be very useful and they may be the most appropriate form of help for many people in many situations. However, a great deal of counselling work goes beyond the brief, focused encounter – it may involve an open-ended relationship developing over a period of months or years.

Sometimes the long-term work has been planned. Both counsellor and client recognise from the outset that the experience, difficulties or curiosity being brought will require lengthy exploration to do them justice; each has the resources and motivation for the work and they agree to undertake it together. Anna, a 34-year-old lecturer, who presented to a counsellor in the health centre of her university with a request for ongoing counselling provides an example of such a situation.

Anna found herself often depressed for no apparent reason and hoped that counselling might help; she had been in counselling before in her early twenties and found it useful. She described how it had been very difficult for her to leave home and establish a life as a more independent person; the previous counselling had helped her separate from her family, especially her mother, whom Anna had experienced as rather intrusive but also as unsure of herself. Without prompting from the counsellor she described a dream where she was in the garden outside a striking house; she was looking towards it, a large double-fronted Victorian villa with beautiful long windows from which drifted the sound of classical music. Despite wishing to go inside she was unable to move to enter the house.

In many ways Anna's life appeared to be going well. She explained that she was making reasonable progress with her research (on domestic architecture) although she was not enjoying it as much as she had. She was unsure of her future career path. She was in a steady and rewarding relationship; her partner wanted to marry and consider starting a family when Anna had completed her book, but she found herself strangely reluctant to make these commitments despite feeling that they were well suited. She wondered aloud if she were really the right kind of person to have a baby and mentioned that she dreamed repeatedly of deformed babies.

The counsellor asked Anna to say a little more about her childhood. She described it as reasonably happy. When the counsellor asked for any special memories Anna described two difficult periods of hospitalisation for severe hip problems and consequent separation from her parents when she was 3 and 6 years old. The first stay in hospital had coincided with the birth of her nearest sibling, a boy. She repeated that she would like counselling to try to understand why she had lost her energy and enthusiasm for moving forward in life.

The counsellor was struck by Anna's view that she needed help with how she felt about herself. It seemed that she had managed her life successfully up to this point. She appeared to be an able member of staff and seemed to be intelligent, sensitive, aware of and interested in the world around her. Anna did not seem totally dependent on one person; she had a number of close friendships as well as the relationship with her partner. Nonetheless Anna was clearly distressed by her inability to settle and make definite commitments to her work or her partner; she seemed unable to believe in herself, take pleasure in her accomplishments or trust her creativity. The counsellor liked Anna, was encouraged by her readiness to communicate her feelings and her dreams and by the fact that she had found her previous counselling helpful. She offered Anna ongoing counselling.

They met for 18 months. Many of the sessions were taken up with Anna's dreams and the shifting states of mind they revealed. Gradually the nightmares about deformed babies became less frequent as Anna and the counsellor explored the meanings of Anna's childhood fears and fantasies. Her early illnesses and enforced hospital stays had left her with a sense of being damaged and not safe to be a mother. She was able to remember the early trauma of being separated from her parents when she was ill and the experience of being sent away to hospital. She had attributed her parents' apparent unwillingness to help her to being her own fault because she had resented the coming of the new baby and been 'a naughty girl'. The dreams about houses continued but began to change. First, Anna was able to enter the house of her dreams although it belonged to someone else; later she dreamed that she owned the house and, in a dream shortly before the counselling ended, she discovered a number of new rooms there. She described a beautiful drawing room complete with antique furniture and a bow window with a view onto a secluded garden and a peaceful galleried library.

At first Anna and her female counsellor were very comfortable together as if settled into an inner courtyard of female intimacy, reminiscent perhaps of the closeness Anna had enjoyed as the first baby with her mother before the intrusion of hospitals and other babies. However, the counsellor's male supervisor drew attention to this cosiness and wondered where the father came into the picture. He suggested that there needed to be some recognition of the frustrating as well as the pleasurable aspects of the counselling. The holiday breaks were very painful for Anna and the counsellor had to be firm with herself to resist making special arrangements for this client by shortening them. Anna was able to acknowledge how dangerous it felt for her to be psychologically separate and yet how necessary this was if she was to develop.

The counselling ended when Anna, having completed her book, left to take up a better post elsewhere. Saying goodbye was very moving and the counsellor felt sad to let go of Anna with whom she had identified so strongly. Anna was feeling much more lively and freer to make choices about a career and the possibility of having a child.

Counselling is not always so successful or so pleasurable, nor is the client always so clear as Anna about wanting help over a period of time. Many people initially consult a counsellor in a state of crisis and upset, hoping that their difficulties will be fairly speedily resolved. They then find themselves becoming more aware of their needs and the rewards of their involvement in the process; they may wish to continue. Others begin by seeking another kind of help and find they are offered and appreciate emotional support and exploration instead of or as well as the more practical help they envisaged. Others come with a seemingly prescribed area of difficulty; often what seems to be a single issue turns out to be merely a conscious or unconscious way through the door and many more issues come to light in the course of exploring the first. In all these situations, once the work has begun, a painful and undigested history, persistent state of mind or difficulty in relating may become apparent; both counsellor and client recognise this – although not necessarily at the same time or to the same extent – and have to reassess their task, abilities and willingness to continue. At this point a referral to another practitioner with more training, experience or time may be appropriate, or necessary because of organisational constraints, but often both counsellor and client prefer to build on an already established relationship; they make a new contract and agree to continue work together with a more open agenda and time scale. There will be further discussion of contracting later. Occasionally too counselling may be long-term by default, not planned or negotiated but dragging on rather aimlessly with neither party quite clear of the purpose. This may be because the counsellor lacks the skills, conviction or confidence to make a timely brief intervention or because either counsellor, client or the pair in collusion is afraid of separating or acknowledging that the work has ceased to be productive.

The 1990s have seen an expansion of counselling provision and a growing number of courses and literature to support a developing profession. This present series of books on professional issues is one indicator of concern with the need for defined standards. The British Association for Counselling (BAC) has established codes of ethics and practice not just for counsellors but also for supervisors and training courses and has produced guidelines for the conduct of research. The setting up of a British register of accredited counsellors is another sign of action around issues of professional legitimacy. In this context of growth and increasing professionalisation we think that it is important to consider specifically the issues raised in long-term counselling. We are not aware of a great deal written specifically on this topic although much of the literature on psychotherapy is clearly relevant; indeed we have drawn on it heavily in writing this book. Some trainings do prepare their students for this kind of work but not all. Many courses offer placements which last no more than a year, hence experience of long-term counselling while training may be limited. Some counsellors train to do a particular kind of work such as marital or bereavement counselling which focuses on one area of difficulty or have experience only in time-limited work and find their own interests and their awareness of clients' needs for a range of interventions expanding over time.

We hope that this book will be of interest to counsellors and that the general reader will also be able to get a sense of the fascination and complexity of counselling from our writing. Many counsellors have already been kind enough to share with us their experience of and thoughts about this work in response to personal requests, letters in *Counselling* and *Counselling News* and enquiries on a World Wide Web e-mail forum. Their thinking has informed ours and some of their views will be quoted later. Correspondence and discussion with colleagues and with each other have helped us to appreciate a diversity of counselling approaches and clarify our commonalties and differences: We will indicate some variety of points of view in the text in the hope of promoting thoughtful discussion. We think our book may be of particular relevance to those who are undertaking or have just completed their initial training and may be embarking on practice for the first time; those whose pattern of work is shifting to include longer contracts with clients; and those whose core training was in a related discipline such as social work but who wish to develop further the coun-selling part of their role.

We do not wish to be overly concerned with hierarchies or professional rivalries. We are not arguing that long-term coun-selling is better or worse than short-term, preferable or inferior to psychotherapy. We believe that long-term work can be rewarding and beneficial for both counsellor and client. It can be a powerful and lasting agent for development and prove lifesaving for some clients. Once weekly long-term work can allow some unstable people to make real changes and prevent others from descending so frequently into psychosis. Sometimes it is the most appropriate and often the only (for geographical or financial reasons) kind of ongoing emotional help available to people in need. The promise of commitment and reliability implied in the counsellor's offer of a long-term and open-ended encounter may allow the client's difficulties to be explored in some depth and worked through; it can allow a relationship to be developed and examined; it can provide the containment necessary for digesting painful experiences and insights into oneself.

On the other hand there are dangers associated with all therapeutic work of whatever length, even in the hands of experienced practitioners. Professionals who have been in practice for some time may forget how powerful and how special the counselling encounter can be for people in distress who may not have much experience of being attended to and taken seriously. Even one session can have a profound impact on a client. A long-term involvement may stir up powerful and difficult to manage feelings about the counsellor; it necessarily risks touching on people's vulnerability, weakening their defences. Not everyone needs or can cope with this and those who do may be harmed by many possible failings in the counsellor – of knowledge, strength, commitment, compassion, boundaries, respect, sensitivity or clear thinking – to name only some. For those who come for or find themselves in a long-term counselling relationship it may be the only opportunity they will have in a lifetime to explore their internal worlds and share deeply personal thoughts and strong feelings. They should be entitled to trained and thoughtful professional helpers.

Counsellors need much more than enthusiasm and the wish to help, although these are good starting points. They need resilience, knowledge about themselves, an understanding of why they do the work, an ability to reflect, to be self-critical and postpone gratification – capacities which should be fostered by training, theory, supervision and therapy. Otherwise they risk confusing their own needs with those of their clients or being unable to sustain the counselling relationship without being submerged in it. They need a conviction of having something worthwhile to offer of themselves and their training if they are to sustain the necessary vicissitudes and self-questioning of long-term engagement. We hope this book will help counsellors consider and make informed judgements about their suitability, motivation and competence for this kind of work and, if they do decide to proceed, to feel more justifiably confident in their practice so that both they and their clients may benefit.

This book will focus on individual therapeutic counselling drawing mainly on the psychodynamic and humanistic traditions and developments of them. Feltham points out that these approaches are 'likely to be more resistant than others to the enforced limits of time' (1997: 28) because of the psychoanalytic emphasis on the importance of early experience and unconscious conflict and the person-centred one on leaving decision-making powers to the client. Counselling in both of these orientations is common in Britain. Other practitioners doing long-term work come from a background in the traditions of gestalt, existential counselling, transactional analysis or psychosynthesis. We are aware that many counsellors are now trained in and use approaches which draw on and integrate aspects of different traditions. We think it would be cumbersome to discuss each issue from the viewpoint of every orientation; hence our choice to focus on the person-centred and the psychodynamic. We hope that integrative counsellors will be able to extrapolate what is relevant to them from our discussions. The more behavioural and cognitive approaches tend to be short-term. The most usual initial offer in cognitive analytic work is 16 sessions (Ryle, 1990). Other behavioural or cognitive approaches would rarely exceed 20 sessions and hence fall outside our definition of long-term. For a discussion of brief dynamic psychotherapy Molnos (1995) is useful, while Feltham (1997) offers a succinct summary of time-limited approaches from a wide range of orientations.

It is hard to define long-term counselling. Rowan (1995) makes the radical suggestion: 'If the contract is open-ended or if there is no contract, that is long-term counselling. It does not then matter how long it lasts.' On the other hand many therapeutic relationships last for several years. Fuller discussion of possible definitions is included in the next chapter, but for the purposes of the book we will assume work of more than 25 sessions while recognising that this would be considered short in some settings such as private practice or a WPF Counselling (formerly Westminster Pastoral Foundation) affiliated or associated centre.

We are aware that counselling takes place in a number of settings. Some organisations offer counselling as a way of supporting their primary task. Hence many universities, colleges and schools, recognising that learning is an emotional as well as intellectual activity, offer their students counselling. GP practices, knowing how many ailments presented to them are at least partly psychological in origin, may employ counsellors to help patients in emotional difficulty. A number of voluntary agencies have a remit to work with particular issues: for example, Cruse works with people who have been bereaved and Victim Support with the emotional responses of crime victims. For some such as social workers counselling is part but not all of their professional role. Many agencies and private practitioners offer general, frequently long-term, open-ended, counselling. The setting in which counsellors work will influence whether or not long-term counselling as we have defined it fits with their own perceptions. Many of the comments and assertions we make in this book refer to the practice of counsellors in the UK. Other cultures may commonly offer only very short-term help and when longer term help is available it may be more usually situated within psychiatric service provision (Sayee Kumar, 1996). We aim to use examples from a range of contexts to illustrate the variety that exists and to indicate how the setting may influence the work.

The next chapter will discuss the parameters of long-term work. Issues of definition, orientation and goals will be considered. We will introduce and elaborate some case histories – based on our own and others' experience of this kind of work although fictionalised to protect confidentiality – to illustrate our sense of who might benefit from long-term counselling and to give some sense of the kind of relationships which may develop and the kind of issues which may arise in long-term work. We will consider the question of assessment from a psychodynamic and person-centred perspective. We will then focus on managing the work and will discuss the issues and day-to-day considerations which arise as the relationship between counsellor and client is established, develops or falters, and ends. We will explore the practical and emotional questions that the counsellor needs to consider in preparing for and sustaining long-term work. Finally, we will discuss the research, evaluation and promotion of this kind of counselling.

2

Parameters

Words and their meanings are never fully fixed in relation to each other: the word counselling being a good example of how the meaning of a term can alter depending on who is using it and which unnamed referents may be framing their thinking. Etymologically, 'counselling' originates from the Latin *consilium* meaning a consultation, through the Old French *conseiller*, meaning to advise and the anglicised word 'counsel', to give advice. Therapeutic counsellors are often concerned to differentiate themselves from advisors, although cognitive-behavioural counsellors recommend certain procedures as part of their work.

Some counsellors are also wary of being identified with the tradition of psychotherapy with its connotations of treatment and psychopathology, while others argue that there are no clearly definable differences between counselling and psychotherapy (Feltham, 1995). Arguably, if counselling and psychotherapy were fully identical then there would be no need to write this book, since most of the very extensive literature on psychotherapy pertains to long-term work. One overwhelming factor which does unite counsellors and psychotherapists who work long-term is the centrality of the therapeutic relationship in bringing about change in the client. This fundamental approach to change also crosses over differences in theoretical orientations and is a potent factor which affects the counsellor or psychotherapist as well as the client, although we might conceive of it differently depending on our training. As well as recognising such common ground, this chapter will look at some ways of defining differences and therefore some ideas about what the specific term 'long-term counselling' can mean. We have used the word client as is customary in the counselling world but do sometimes quote from writers who prefer to describe those receiving therapeutic help as patients.

However, it is not the intention of the authors to produce a categorisation which 'works' for everyone in every situation. Indeed, the writers themselves do not necessarily agree with each other about every point made in this chapter or elsewhere in the book. We are however in complete agreement about the importance of maintaining professional standards in any therapeutic work and the desirability of greater clarity about the kind of help which is on offer so that potential clients may be protected from poor practice and given the opportunity to make an informed choice. What follows is one attempt to establish some criteria for defining 'long-term counselling' for the purposes of this book, but it is up to the readers to judge whether or not the framework permits them to think about the issues which have led them to pick up the book in the first place.

The chapter will also go on to consider the nature of goals in long-term counselling and how they differ not only with each client but in different theoretical orientations, although here, too, we will find much which is shared. The rationale behind our choice to define long-term as 25 sessions and over will also be explained. We hope we can help people provide long-term help to others that is both successful from the client's point of view and rewarding for the counsellor. In our attempt to outline the parameters of long-term counselling we explore it as a topic of practical interest rather than a theoretically clear-cut area.

Defining the kind of work we mean

Long-term approaches to helping people which fall within the remit of this book are all based on the centrality of the helping relationship in either bringing about change or preventing deterioration. However, there are related activities which are informal and extremely useful but which we will not address. One such approach is befriending, which is often on a very long-term basis and possibly shares some of the characteristics which we outline here but not enough of them for us to include it within the remit of this book. Nor do we offer advice to those numerous professionals who take a counselling approach to their work but essentially see their roles as fitting with the skill requirements of a particular profession, for example, nursing or social work. However, in situations when such people use counselling as their main approach to helping and define their other professional role as secondary, then we feel we have something to offer.

Another long-term approach is psychotherapy and it is on this borderline delineation that much controversy occurs. Thorne has described the danger of trying to clarify the differences between counselling and psychotherapy, using the language of warfare to evoke his fears: 'I sense . . . a metaphorical battlefield where lines are being drawn up and where forces of violent destructiveness go about their sinister missions cloaked in the garments of standards, qualifications and concern for the public good' (1992: 244). Such strength of feeling is not uncommon. However, it may be the case that thinking through the relatively uncharted territory of the field of counselling and psychotherapy stirs up intense theoretical and philisophical passions as well as competitiveness and rivalry which can of course prompt positive as well as negative endeavours.

Some differences between counsellors and psychotherapists have been proposed such as how many sessions a week are offered to a client (Jacobs, 1988) or the setting in which the client presents for help (Einzig, 1989). Trainings too may differ, though both counselling and psychotherapy vary in length with the latter tending towards 4 years part-time for many but not all trainings. The need for personal therapy to counteract 'contamination' is seen as de rigueur in most but not all psychotherapy training and in some but not all counselling. A survey by the British Association for Counselling (BAC, 1993) in which a total of 2,500 question-naires were sent out to the whole membership revealed that members spent an average of 2.5 years in part-time training and that personal therapy was a requirement in 41 per cent of courses. In the survey, 500 completed questionnaires were selected for analysis out of the 53 per cent of questionnaires returned. The 500 analysed questionnaires represent only a fifth of BAC member-ship and the statistics must be treated therefore with some caution. BAC does require experience of personal counselling for the purposes of counsellor accreditation. As from 1998, the minimum requirement will be 40 hours of personal counselling or equivalent consistent with the counselling model that is espoused by the counsellor. WPF Counselling, the largest provider of training for long-term counselling in the UK, requires those training part-time to attend for 5 years and be in personal therapy for at least the last four of these before the award of independent practitioner status. Thus, despite the BAC accreditation scheme for courses there are considerable differences between counselling trainings and place-ment experiences which may be addressed as the Counselling Register develops. Such discrepancies are no doubt due partly to the difficulties likely to arise in an emerging profession.

Precise information about psychotherapists is not available yet as the UK Council for Psychotherapy (UKCP) collects information through its member groups and details about personal therapy and training are not collected centrally (at the time of writing this book). However, UKCP has recently extended the recommended length of training from 3 to 4 years part-time as a requirement for member-ship to its sections, in the light of European Association of Psycho-therapy guidelines. Personal therapy is not a requirement of some psychotherapy trainings such as cognitive-behavioural psycho-therapy. A perusal of the Universities Psychotherapy Association Review (Pearmain, 1996) suggests that trainings in universities vary from 2.5 to 5 years part-time in length and that all stipulate trainees should be in personal therapy, though varying in recommended lengths and frequencies.

What exactly these unsystematic findings reveal is unclear but it does seem likely that, on average, counsellors and psychotherapists have slightly different lengths of trainings and a different degree of emphasis on the desirability of personal therapy. However, the differences between counsellors and psychotherapists are no greater than between the requirements for different forms of psychotherapy training. Struggles over status and earning power, which are linked to questions of training, can be impediments to clear thinking about how to differentiate constructively but are part and parcel of the development of professional roles. The newly emerging profession of counselling psychology is engaged in a similar attempt to clarify the role of the counselling psychologist (see James and Palmer, 1996) and has to battle with similar issues but with the added ingredient of several competing psychology specialisms. Dryden leavens the debate with a touch of humour when he answers the question of what is the difference between a counsellor and a psychotherapist with the answer 'about £8,000' (1996: 29). Parry carried out a review of psychological therapies in the National Health Service and found similar problems there with: 'widespread confusion about psychotherapy. The terms "psycho-logical therapy", "psychotherapy", "counselling", "specialised psy-chotherapy", "psychological treatment", "trained psychotherapist" are used unsystematically and with different meanings' (1996: 5).

Having tried to initiate a discussion at an informal level on the Internet about how counsellors and psychotherapists differ from each other, the authors were staggered by the disagreement that reigned. The international (but English-speaking) discussion that ensued was lively and stimulating, but many participants seemed unable to divorce their views about the differences or similarities from their opinions about the efficacy of different models. All the comments were interesting and Hermansson (1996) offered a good summing up of the three main alternatives which are proposed by Belkin (1988: 22) as:

- no difference between the two;
- difference based on theoretical foundations, practical concerns and discrepant historical origins;
- difference based on seriousness of presenting problems and 'emotional depth' of or 'intensity' of the treatment.

However, there was literally no agreement about which of these three held more validity. Furthermore, there was a great deal of discussion about whether orientation should be either disclosed or adhered to in responding to the needs of clients. The following is an extract from the debate by an American participant which shows what American counsellors face in relation to health insurance schemes and which makes orientation more problematic for them than the counselling–psychotherapy divide discussed here:

> Another reason I see people identifying orientation is with managed care providers who ASK assertively! If you are psychodynamic or psychoanalytic in your theoretical approach, you are practically guaranteed NOT to be considered a provider. They are very assertive here about wanting cognitive-behavioural, short-term, brief therapy. Period. (Ward, 1996)

The field of counselling and psychotherapy

Some individuals associated with organisations that have provided psychological help and professional therapeutic training in Britain have proposed their own criteria. Brown and Pedder (1991) set out a clear way of separating psychotherapy into different levels which draws on the work of Cawley (1977). Their definitions are taught to medical students and their book is on the reading lists for many

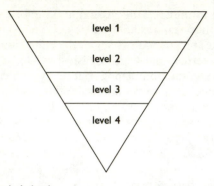

Figure 2.1 *Cawley's levels*
Source: Cawley, 1977

psychotherapy training courses. It is written from the point of view
of psychiatrists who are also psychoanalysts and therefore it takes
as its reference points medicine and psychoanalysis, neither of
which is an automatic reference point for all counsellors.

Nevertheless, Brown and Pedder outline useful categories which
can be modified for those who do not see counselling from such a
particular angle. It seems important to start from the definitions that
already exist rather than try to concoct them without reference to
some powerful agencies that have already made distinctions.
Unfortunately, Brown and Pedder make uncritical use of Cawley's
concept of levels, despite 12 years (1979–91) elapsing between
the first and second editions of their book, a time in which counselling has flourished. This notion of levels immediately orders the
reader's thinking in a hierarchical fashion implying that what is at
the top is the most expert and best and this is bound to cause
offence. In Cawley's case the pyramid of hierarchy is pointing from
surface to depth so that Level 1 is the top with the gradient sloping
down to greater 'depth' (see Figure 2.1). Again, this is sure to
annoy many people who carry out excellent work at this 'level' and
do not feel properly respected by such a metaphor.

At Level 1 is placed the approach that nowadays is often associated with the use of counselling skills, rather than counselling per
se: 'It involves an awareness of the person as well as the problem
he presents, and requires an ability to communicate and empathise
with people from different backgrounds' (Brown and Pedder,
1991: 88).

Level 2 is described as being 'what a good psychiatrist, social worker or psychologist does' – this includes the skills previously mentioned but with an added sensitivity to factors outside the patient's awareness or control which may affect his or her behaviour. An ability to communicate with people suffering from all sorts of psychological disturbance is a further aspect of Level 2 psychotherapy. Transference is recognised but not worked with, apart from the fostering of a mildly positive transference to the practitioner.

Level 3 is designated 'what many people mean by psychotherapy' (ibid.: 89) and includes the previous levels in terms of respect, understanding and acceptance of the patient but also encompasses some confrontation of the patient's defences or targets deficits. Brown and Pedder go on to centre the fulcrum of change in the patient–practitioner relationship and the use of psychodynamic principles such as interpretation of unconscious conflicts, dreams and transference material as the means by which change is brought about. This last aspect of Level 3 psychotherapy is also carried out in psychodynamic counselling, but not in humanistic or behavioural counselling which does not espouse interpretation as a strategy for change.

Level 4 is designated as a behavioural approach to manifest problems in the patient's learned behaviour and therapy is seen as a re-education of the patient through adopting better or more 'adaptive' coping mechanisms.

Although these levels fail adequately to represent the range of approaches offered by psychotherapists and counsellors in the present period they may establish a baseline from which to constitute criteria for both length and type of psychological and emotional help. The Level 4 category is oddly placed in our mind at the apex of the pyramid since it is concerned with more concrete entities in terms of both symptom or distress and intervention. Indeed, Brown and Pedder proceed to leave to one side this aspect of psychotherapy and concentrate instead on the first three levels. Nonetheless, their work permits us to develop a revised category based on economic use of clusters of interventions (see Table 2.2). If Level 1 skills are sufficient to help someone then a practical, conscientious person with active listening skills and the ability to empathise and understand another person is all that is needed. This is not formal counselling but includes the use of counselling skills and involves personal qualities which are precious to any helper.

If the cluster of abilities includes more refinement of the skills previously mentioned and additional strengths in relation to interviewing and communicating with a wider range of people in distress then, again, counselling training may be desirable but is not absolutely necessary (see Kagan, 1980). It is only when the idea of a contract for change comes onto the agenda and the relationship itself is highlighted that both therapeutic counselling and psychotherapy come into focus. So far then it can be argued that Levels 1 and 2 describe trained professionals who use counselling skills as part of their repertoire of techniques to help another person in some kind of trouble. We will call these two levels Cluster 1 and Cluster 2 since they seem to describe attributes and abilities which are extremely desirable in any helper. The notion of clusters of skills takes the emphasis away from hierarchical schemas, though there is still a risk of reproducing the same problem but on the plane of number of skills.

When the practitioner's intent is to bring about change in the other by using the skills described and via the medium of the relationship, then a third area has been established which includes both counselling and psychotherapy. Skills used in this domain will depend on the orientation of the counsellor or psychotherapist. Before elaborating further, a return to Brown and Pedder is helpful because they go on to set out aspects of counselling and psychotherapy which are useful, even though some readers may be alienated by this continued stress on patients and practitioners which is the discourse of the medical model. Cawley's levels have been adapted by Brown and Pedder as shown in Table 2.1.

Clusters of skills and interventions

Table 2.1 may be helpful to those psychodynamic practitioners who feel they work at several of these levels. In such cases, according to Cawley (1977), they would at times be providing psychotherapy and not counselling. Another important factor needs to be added to the schema which is the formal contracting of a therapeutic agenda, be it counselling or psychotherapy. A key point is when a contract is set up to bring about a change in the client by means of counselling or psychotherapy. We would also prefer to adapt the list somewhat as it shifts perspective at point 5, at times bringing in what the practitioner does rather than the client. It may be necessary for non-psychoanalytically based

Table 2.1 *Cawley's levels as adapted by Brown and Pedder*

Level 1 'Outer' or support and counselling
1 Unburdening of problems to sympathetic listener
2 Ventilation of feelings within supportive relationship

Level 2 'Intermediate'
3 Discussion of problems with non-judgemental helper
4 Clarification of problems, their nature and origins, within deepening relationship
5 Confrontation of defences

Level 3 'Deeper' or exploration and analysis
6 Interpretation of unconscious motives and transference phenomena
7 Repetition, remembering and reconstruction of the past
8 Regression to less adult way of functioning
9 Resolution of conflicts by re-experiencing and working them through within the therapeutic relationship

Source: Brown and Pedder, 1991

psychotherapies to map out how their work develops after this point. The language of Cawley, Brown and Pedder may also strike a jarring note for practising counsellors, especially those working from a humanistic perspective. We would propose the following amendments as shown in Table 2.2.

We can now envisage both psychotherapists and counsellors as working within a given area but with counsellors identified as focusing their efforts mainly on work with non-regressed aspects of the client across a range of interventions from point 1 to point 8; each counsellor being trained to different levels of expertise and competence and different orientations attributing therapeutic value to different clusters.

This also accommodates those who tend to see psychotherapy as about sessions that often take place more than once a week since the increased frequency may indicate a greater likelihood of regression. Counsellors may see clients more frequently than once a week, though this is not prevalent and may not necessarily coincide with an increased attention to Cluster 3 interventions. Extra sessions in themselves do not signify a change though they may represent a consequence of an altered emphasis in the approach of the counsellor – it really depends on what is done in the session. On the other hand, regression work carried out in primal therapy, for instance, would not necessarily involve more frequent sessions, nor does it always in analytic therapy. The

Table 2.2 *Clusters of interventions*

Cluster 1   Support using counselling skills

The use of attending and listening skills within a supportive relationship to facilitate:

1   the unburdening of problems by the client or patient
2   the expression of feelings

Cluster 2   Establishing counselling

The formally contracted use of therapeutic and relationship skills to facilitate:

3   exploration of problems or feelings within a non-judgemental relationship
4   clarification of problems or feeling-states, their nature and origins, within a deepening relationship
5   interventions aimed at lowering defences or changing preconceptions and self-defeating behaviour

Cluster 3   Further exploration and psychotherapy

The use of interventions in a supportive but also challenging relationship including:

6   interpretation of unconscious or pre-conscious material and transference phenomena
7   facilitation of repetition, remembering and reconstruction of the past
8   resolution of conflicts by enabling re-experiencing and working through within the therapeutic relationship
9   permission and acceptance of regression to less adult way of functioning in the client and interventions addressed to the regressed or psychotic part of the patient's mind

---

framework will not cover every eventuality for counsellors but it gives us the opportunity to begin to think about the opportunities and limits of long-term counselling.

The cluster model also offers a more musical metaphor: the counsellor may well place the downbeat on the first four or five areas of skills while able to entertain the whole musical scale, whereas the psychotherapist plays mainly at the other end of the scale. Jacobs (1994: 86) conceptualised clusters of practice in a similar way, though he used personal construct theory to produce the idea of a counselling–psychotherapy map.

This simple description is for the purposes of this book. The Advice, Guidance, Counselling and Psychotherapy Lead Body (AGCPLB) is attempting a more thoroughgoing analysis in order to set standards for NVQs. BAC and UKCP, but not BCP, are contributing to this undertaking. The fruits of the debate which has started have yet to be harvested in terms of clear definitions of 'competencies' (a problematic word, in our view, which flattens all the efforts of counsellors and psychotherapists to bring finesse and sensitivity to their work) and so are not available for integration into this book.

So far, a notion of the counsellor using a cluster of skills for clients who respond in the fairly classic way described above brings psychodynamic counselling into focus but leaves person-centred counsellors only at the threshold of this view of a shared world of psychotherapy and counselling. Cognitive-behavioural methods of helping people would (apart from cognitive analytic therapy, CAT) also eschew a need to 'descend' to Level 3 or use the clusters of skills involved in that area though 'working through' in the ordinary sense of the term is a necessary aspect of cognitive-behavioural approaches. Such approaches would be anchored in the cluster of skills of point 5: challenging defences or maladaptive responses. This is where the weaknesses in Cawley's classification and Brown and Pedder's revision of it become apparent. In person-centred counselling the reference points are not medicine or psychoanalysis and the differentiation from psychotherapy is not simply at the level of skills, approaches or choice of patients but involves a much more fundamental objection to the values implicit in the patient–therapist construct.

Where does person-centred counselling fit in?

Thorne's concerns about a 'hidden agenda' in distinguishing different practices are rooted in the treatment meted out decades ago to Carl Rogers by American psychiatrists who tried to stop him operating a counselling centre at the University of Chicago. However, as Thorne points out, similar restrictive practices still operate in many parts of Europe and the European Association of Psychotherapists seems keen to repeat history, but this time with psychiatrists and psychologists united against everyone else. Thorne's survey of extant attempts to delineate the two professions from each other pokes fun at the idea that counselling is, on the whole, for less disturbed people, dealing with conscious problems and requiring a single-issue focus while psychotherapy is for more disturbed people who exhibit less apparent constellations of problems. Thorne rejects what is true for some counselling on the basis that it is not true for all counselling. This limits the structuring of a differential classification. It would, for example, be wrong to suggest that an advice worker simply tells a client what to do while a counsellor provides an emotional climate in which clients make their own decisions. The differences between the two related approaches to the client are not so simple but at the same time they are real.

Short shrift is also given by Thorne to any stress on the goals or the kind of client who is seen in counselling as an indicator of the differences between counselling and psychotherapy. He also criticises those people he calls 'overlappers'. This is a reference to those who, like Cawley, propose a continuum with counsellors at one end and psychotherapists at the opposite end. The notion of clusters is, we hope, not exactly the same as a continuum, but it is in a similar vein. Clusters permit a field of therapeutic help to be envisaged where different perspectives can be entertained and yet where there are some distinctions between the perspectives. This allows us also to consider the possibility that counselling often leads into psychotherapy (see Jacobs, 1994) and that the job title of the practitioner does not necessarily describe the work done – counsellors may practise psychotherapy at times and psychotherapists may sometimes be counselling. Some counsellors will, no doubt, be objecting that so far, the person-centred approach is not easily fitted into a framework so shaped by psychoanalytic precepts.

Rogers (1951) makes a strong argument about his fundamental disagreement with the interpretive approach of psychoanalytically based therapies and their imputed tendency to make happen what is expected to happen (such as dependency and transference of infantile feelings to the therapist). Rogers also categorised many of the interventions made in interviews as either subtly or directly evaluative of the client and noted that such a manner of relating would make a client defensive, especially towards the counsellor. To stay at points 1 to 4 in Table 2.2 would not simply be efficient or ecological but a mark of the person-centred approach according to Rogers' account of person-centred therapy. In this respect, providing that points 1 to 4 are embedded in the core conditions of acceptance, empathic understanding and congruency (Rogers, 1990b: 136), then the use of other clusters of skills or qualities would be representative of a move away from his preferred approach rather than a 'deepening' of the relationship.

Another aspect of classification is the issue of 'cure'. Psychotherapy is a form of treatment which implies a form of cure.

Psychoanalysis on the other hand, though offering a possibility of 'cure', is also considered an experience in itself and worth doing for the prophylactic benefits and insights that it brings. Counselling too has been considered as not necessarily linked to a concept of 'cure'. Rogers writes:

> This does not mean that it [client-centred therapy] will cure every psychological condition, and indeed the concept of cure is quite foreign to the approach we have been considering . . . Yet a psychological climate which the individual can use for deeper self-understanding, for a reorganisation of self in the direction of more realistic integration, for the development of more comfortable and mature ways of behaving – this is not an opportunity which is of use for some groups and not for others. It would appear to be rather a point of view which might in basic ways be applicable to all individuals, even though it might not resolve all the problems or provide all the help which a particular individual needs. (Rogers, 1951: 230)

In the quotation from Rogers there is a hint of the values inherent in the person-centred approach, which though based on different beliefs are akin to the merits sometimes claimed for psychoanalysis. Curiously, this brings the person-centred approach, in some limited respects, closer to psychoanalysis than to more directive and goal-oriented approaches. Perhaps there is a dimension missing from the clusters mentioned that can never be comfortably placed in this framework and which may have to remain outside the remit of this book although it infuses the outlook of every long-term counsellor or psychotherapist. This dimension goes beyond utilitarian goals to the prizing of the very process of self-discovery and reflection by both counsellors and psychotherapists.

Rogers consistently used the terms counselling and psychotherapy interchangeably as far as we have been able to see. His pleas for a non-directive therapy which was not medically based and which has commonly become known as counselling suggest that person-centred counsellors may feel it reasonable to be described as working in non-confrontational ways with the clusters of skills and attitudinal qualities which belong to points 1–4. This is important for several reasons, not least of which is that it suggests a possible option for those people who require a supportive approach and who may be unable to cope with other kinds of interventions. However, it does not follow that person-centred counsellors are not working at 'depth' or with people who do not have severe difficulties to face. It does mean that they occupy a unique position in that they may steer away from the kinds of interventions which other orientations valorise when they judge what is psychotherapy and what is counselling. The most important issue for this book is that an attempt to delineate counselling from psychotherapy should emphasise the central point that some people benefit from long-term counselling and some people do not. Counsellors need to know when and how to draw the line about what they can and cannot do with different clients.

Goals

The goals of long-term counselling will vary with each client and in different orientations. As mentioned earlier, the person-centred approach does not easily fit into a framework that is based on psychopathology and its treatments. The person-centred counsellor may aim for the facilitation of the client's potential for self-actualisation in long-term counselling in principle, but will do so by following the client's agenda in practice. This is an important distinction for person-centred counsellors who do not set a concrete goal if it means moving away from the frame of reference of the client. It is difficult to consider the end objective of counselling as separate from the process of creating the core conditions. Rogers calls this an 'if–then' variety of theory (1990a) and suggests: 'There is no clear distinction between process and outcome.' The changes he goes on to list include greater congruence and openness to experiences with less defensive behaviour and an improved ability to solve problems. The client's psychological adjustment will be 'closer to the optimum' (ibid.: 241) and he will have improved self-regard. Furthermore, his perceptions will be more realistic and accurate which will make him more accepting of others and also able to take responsibility for himself. Rogers concludes: 'As a consequence . . . his behaviour is more creative, more uniquely adaptive to each new situation, and each new problem, more fully expressive of his own purposes and values' (ibid.: 242).

A psychodynamically orientated counsellor may also hope for the outcome of the counselling relationship to be along similar lines. It is difficult to imagine any counsellor or psychotherapist disagreeing with Roger's heartfelt expression of how he saw the 'fully-functioning person' becoming able to lead a life which: 'involves the courage to be. It means launching oneself fully into the stream of life' (1990a: 240). However, someone with a psycho-dynamic background may also see resolution of conflicts, reduction of symptoms or improvement of the individual's capacity to manage his or her life as goals to target, with reference to the particular developmental stage of the client. The gaining of insight into oneself and others is a desirable outcome and a goal to be aimed for but may not be synonymous with a successful resolution of the counselling relationship. Perhaps both person-centred and psychodynamic counsellors share the expectation that they will go as far as they can towards helping their clients to live more successfully without striving after the perfection of a 'fully-functioning' person or the chimera of a fully mature and conflict-free individual.

It is with the cognitive-behavioural approach that the setting of goals becomes much clearer and more limited. Counsellors who work in this orientation collaborate with clients to define the problems they wish to work on and set about trying to help the client make the necessary changes which they have identified. These may involve understanding and changing both irrational thoughts and counterproductive behaviour though the consequences may go beyond these to transform the client's whole life. Taking a long time to resolve problems may be conceived more readily to be a sign of inefficiency or poor skill in this way of working. Some relatively short-term approaches such as cognitive analytic therapy (CAT), though restricted to 16 sessions with another 8 added on in certain circumstances (Ryle et al., 1994), try to make sense of the complicated problems they address and have elaborate methods of dealing with them. CAT practitioners may spend several hours working out formulations, diagrams and goodbye letters which they give to their clients. Such interventions are time-consuming and demand a good deal of creative thinking on the part of the professional as well as making the client work very hard in the sessions. Normally, such 'value-added' extras are not counted in with the time taken to deliver the sessions in person, but if they were included it is quite possible that CAT would no longer be seen as quite so short-term. Indeed, McCormick (1994: 190) has suggested that CAT practitioners in private practice should charge more per session than they would normally since the work involved between sessions is so extensive and the session itself makes greater demands on the therapist than long-term work.

How long is long-term?

A survey by BAC (1993) discovered that most parties in the 500 completed questionnaires selected for analysis saw clients for an average length of 11.8 sessions of 1.04 hours each. They discovered that most counsellors saw people for contracts that peaked at 1–6 sessions or 11–25 sessions. Organisations that took part saw a ceiling of 25 sessions as normal. The Association for Student Counselling has discovered four to be the average number of sessions for clients seen in student counselling centres (Phippen, 1994) though many services see a minority of clients for a number of years, sometimes up to and beyond the end of their course. WPF Counselling offers the majority of its clients open-ended work and a substantial minority is seen for more than two years, although this may change. Some other agencies set a two-year limit. Employee Assistance Programmes according to Feltham (1997) see clients for between 3 and 8 sessions on average. The setting in which a counsellor works will obviously affect how lengthy long-term actually means. A curious feature of both counselling and psychotherapy is that their origins are in brief contracts but they have evolved into longer term contracts and are now currently faced with pressures to reduce the length of time it takes to reach a satisfactory outcome.

The decision we have made to classify long-term work is rather arbitrary as there is a rapidly changing therapeutic climate in which short has become too long. For example, Malan's influential work on brief dynamic therapy (1963) aimed at treatment within a regime of up to approximately 40 sessions. The emphasis has shifted to extremely short sessions such as the two-plus-one session model (Barkham, 1989) or even one-off sessions as proposed by Talmon (1990) in his 'Single Session Therapy' model. You will have noticed that the length of the sessions has not prevented them from being designated as therapy by their advocates and not counselling or treatment.

For the purposes of this book we mean over 25 sessions for long-term work, since this goes beyond the average number of counselling sessions recorded by BAC and is also longer than the most fast-growing short-term therapy in the UK (CAT) which offers up to 16 sessions. We fully recognise that this represents very short-term work in psychodynamically orientated counselling and therapy. We view less than 6 sessions as short-term counselling and 6 to 25 sessions as medium-term counselling. The lower limit of 25 sessions gives the reader a picture of a client who will be seen for more than half the year, with all the implications of breaks and changes which that implies. However, it is probably important to remember that not all contracts are made with an end number of sessions in mind, so we are speaking both of sessions that are expected to go on for more than six months but also sessions where the termination date is not clear at the outset in the mind of the counsellor and the contract is open-ended. We would also add that we have in mind a continuous period of counselling and not an intermittent sequence of contracts, although the counselling may indeed fall into phases when the contract is re-evaluated.

Conclusion

The differences between behaviourally based approaches and others seem to exemplify the central concerns which long-term work addresses. On the whole, time is considered necessary as a factor in itself for both psychodynamic and person-centred approaches to take root. The brief focused ways of working instituted by Malan (1963, 1976), Mann (1973) and Molnos (1995) all take time even though they are 'focused' on particular essential problems. It may be that 'working through' can be speeded up and may be limited to key areas alone (as is often the case in long-term work) but it cannot by definition be instantaneous.

A very skilled person-centred practitioner may be able to establish the core conditions with a client very rapidly, as Rogers plainly could (but clients still have to find their own way of making use of the resources to hand). It is this attitude towards time which is so important in positioning longer term ways of working, not as luxurious or lazy options, or out-of-focus methods but as the positive marriage of time and a therapeutic relationship to work towards satisfactory change. Time is never unlimited but it is one of the commitments made and protected in a contract for long-term counselling. Long-term counselling goes against the contemporary trend whereby: 'On the social scale, by inventing technologies that bring whatever it is we want to us, and which do so immediately, we are abolishing time' (Brennan, 1993: 175). Counselling can bring some immediate relief but time itself is required before changes can be really tested and secured.

The issue of whether or not individuals or agencies should pay for approaches which take time seems to be almost entirely economic and it is to be expected that they will encourage service deliverers to make efficient use of time. This does not mean long-term counselling contracts should be seen as a sign of failure or, just as wrongly, as defined by contrast with short-term approaches to helping people. Recent research (Chiesa et al., 1996) has demonstrated that it is cost effective for some people to receive long-term help. Similarly, Seligman (1996) found that those clients who received more than six months' help felt that they did better than those who received less, especially if they were deemed as suffering from severe problems. More discussion of the research issues involved in long-term counselling will be found in Chapter 7.

It is therefore wise to bear in mind the kind of client who may enter counselling as well as the method of counselling when thinking about which situations distinguish long-term work as a suitable option. As Barkham suggests:

> While findings indicate that for many clients the greater impact of counselling or therapy occurs during the initial time frame, with subsequent gains requiring more time, for many clients, especially those who have been severely damaged, effective therapeutic work may not be possible until considerable work has been carried out in establishing, for example, an effective therapeutic alliance. What this means is that there are clients for whom briefer therapies are appropriate and clients for whom longer therapies are appropriate. The issue is to determine what is best for each client. (Barkham, 1996: 337)

The clients themselves will be discussed in the next chapter.

3

Who Might Benefit?

In this chapter we should like to introduce some characters who will reappear in later chapters. The people we describe might all, we think, benefit from long-term counselling. These portraits are intended to enliven and illustrate our thinking and allow readers to form their own opinions. The clients described here are imaginary. We have drawn on our experience with real clients but – for reasons of confidentiality – the people here are composites rather than disguised portraits. We have tried to give some indication of the range of clients, issues and settings with which counsellors may work and some of the difficulties they may encounter. Our aim is not to prescribe a right approach or particular orientation but to point to some questions the long-term counsellor may wish to ask. Readers are invited to bring their own experiences and theoretical concerns to a consideration of whether each of the clients we describe may – or may not – need long-term work and of the ways in which the counsellor was – or was not – helpful to the client.

Pamela Jones

Scene One

It is 9.30 on Monday morning at an inner city general medical practice. This practice offers a drop-in surgery on a first-come, first-served basis in the mornings. Today the surgery is very busy. About twenty-five people are waiting to see one of three doctors. Among them is 37-year-old Pamela Jones. After an hour's wait it is her turn. She has waited longer to see her usual doctor.

Her distress is apparent as soon as she enters the consulting room. She looks as if she has been crying and hasn't slept. The doctor enquires about the problem. Pamela explains that her daughter, Marie, and she have had a furious row on Saturday night. The 18 year old has told her mother she is pregnant. Pamela, herself a lone parent, has been horrified. The daughter has left the house and not been in contact since. Pamela is distraught. She asks the doctor to tell her where the girl is.

The GP is taken aback. He doesn't know where Marie is, nor that she is pregnant, although she too is one of his patients. Even if he did know her whereabouts he would not be free to tell Pamela. When he tells Pamela this she is uncomprehending: she is the girl's mother, Marie is her only child, surely the doctor knows that she has her daughter's best interests at heart, surely he too is concerned about this young girl's situation.

The doctor is torn. This surgery is supposed to be for quick consultations, for people who cannot wait for a regular, more leisurely appointment. Pamela is very distressed but she is not ill. He is tempted to tell her not to worry, Marie will doubtless be back soon, to go home and try to get some rest. However, he knows that Pamela has a history of depression; in the past he has suggested she see the practice counsellor but Pamela has refused the offer, preferring anti-depressants to help her keep going with looking after her child and her job as a legal receptionist. He repeats gently but firmly that of course he is concerned for Marie and of course he will offer her medical care and advice should she consult him, but he has to respect her confidentiality as that of any other patient. He allows Pamela time to protest and to express her huge worries about her daughter and eventually finds a way of saying that he is concerned for the mother too as this is obviously going to be a very difficult period in her life. He himself does not have all the time she may need and asks her to reconsider seeing the counsellor.

Reluctantly Pamela agrees to give it a try. By good luck the receptionist discovers that the counsellor has a space in two days' time because of a cancellation and Pamela accepts this along with an information sheet about counselling.

Scene Two
Wednesday afternoon in the counselling room at the practice. The counsellor, who has trained in person-centred counsel-

ling but is also familiar with the psychodynamic approach and has considerable experience with clients, is waiting for Pamela and reflecting on what the GP has told her about the client. Pamela is late and the counsellor wonders if she will come at all, knowing what she does of her reluctance and suspecting that Pamela may feel rejected by the doctor's attempt to hand her over to the counsellor. She wonders about the relationship between mother and daughter and what it might mean that the daughter seems to be repeating history by becoming pregnant at the same age as her mother. Fifteen minutes into the session time Pamela arrives.

Pamela begins rather guardedly saying she is not sure what she is supposed to say or why the doctor thought counselling would help — what she needs is her daughter back. The counsellor explains that there are no right and wrong things to talk about although she can't counsel the daughter indirectly; perhaps they can discover whether they can help the mother deal with her dismaying experience. She would like to know more about Pamela's history and sense of herself but, feeling the pressure of Pamela's immediate concern, instead asks her about news of Marie. Pamela is even more distraught than on Monday. She describes a series of unsuccessful attempts to trace Marie and demands to know if her daughter has contacted the practice, if she should go back to the police who have so far been unhelpful, what she can have done to deserve this, whether the counsellor has children and can understand how she feels. The counsellor says very little but registers in herself how panic stricken and helpless Pamela feels. She conveys her interest and concern by listening attentively and empathising with Pamela's extreme anxiety about her daughter. As time runs out she decides to offer Pamela another appointment, thinking that counselling might provide the containment Pamela will need to help her manage her overpowering feelings over the next period. Pamela agrees to return.

Scene Three
When she does, arriving on time on this occasion, she looks much better. Marie has returned home, there has been a reconciliation, they will bring up the baby together. She says she has come back only to thank the counsellor for her time

the previous week. The counsellor thinks all may not continue as idyllically as Pamela hopes; she knows that thanks could have been conveyed by phone or letter and yet Pamela has chosen to come in person. She suggests that they use the time which has been set aside for the meeting to find out more about Pamela and the force of her reaction to the row with her daughter. She wonders aloud about the relationship between Pamela and her own mother.

It turns out that much of Pamela's childhood has been spent in care. Her own mother had been extremely unreliable and had left her in the care of Social Services on many occasions but would never agree to an adoption. Pamela has tried to give her own daughter all the mothering she never had. The rupture with her daughter has revived all her feelings of abandonment and worthlessness. She is terrified of losing her daughter around whom her whole life revolves and says she can foresee no difficulties in sharing the care for the new baby.

The counsellor can imagine many difficulties and she suggests that Pamela might like the opportunity to talk about her feelings about herself as mother, daughter and grand-mother to be. Pamela looks both surprised and relieved at this offer, says she's felt better for 'the chat' and agrees to come regularly for the next couple of months as soon as the counsellor has an ongoing space available. They agree to review the situation after two months.

The ongoing work
At this point the counsellor wants to offer help but is not yet sure whether a longer term contract is appropriate. She is aware of the extent of Pamela's neediness and fears for her pain if the daughter manages to separate and live her own life, but she is not yet sure what kind of counselling this new client can sustain and thinks Pamela is not in a position to be clear about what she wants for herself as counselling is so unfamiliar to her. The counsellor's own situation is different from Pamela's; she has done considerable work on her rela-tionship with her own mother in her own completed coun-selling and this helps her be aware of the possibility of being overly identified with her new client. She is nonetheless con-scious of a pull to be overprotective and overinvolved out of

a wish to compensate Pamela for her missing mother and partner.

After an irregular beginning Pamela does settle into coming to most of her once weekly counselling sessions. She develops a friendly and open attitude towards the counsellor but makes little use of any comments that the counsellor makes about Pamela's relationship to or feelings about her which are always brushed aside. In most sessions she talks about what Marie has done and how she has reacted but occasionally she talks of her own childhood and how awful she has felt. At the review Pamela says it has been helpful to talk about her daughter and asks to continue until after the birth. The counsellor agrees to this.

There follows a stormy period during which Pamela relives much of her own unsupported pregnancy and, with the counsellor's help, struggles to let her daughter make her own choices. She is nonetheless devastated when her daughter does move away with the new baby. At this point the counsellor chooses to offer Pamela an open-ended contract because she is aware of the extent of her client's need and because Pamela has been able to use sessions to explore her feelings and problems and think about her usual way of relating. The counsellor explains that she is willing to work with Pamela as long as they both thnk it useful and that they will agree a date for ending together. Pamela accepts.

The work is quite slow; the counsellor had hoped to help Pamela understand herself more fully by exploring the relationship between her history and her current feelings and her conflicting feelings about being dependent on the counsellor, particularly in the light of her parents' unreliability. She hopes that Pamela may be able to resolve some of her conflicts about risking mature dependency on another human being by re-experiencing and working these through in the therapeutic relationship. Sometimes Pamela can make links between her past and her current feelings about herself, her daughter and her counsellor but she often prefers to avoid thinking about her past or her feelings about the counsellor too much and may miss a session after one which has felt too upsetting to her. Gradually, however, she becomes more able to bear her recollections of her painful early experience and to recognise similar feelings when they are stirred up in the present.

The ending
The counselling lasts for two and a half years in all. By then Pamela, although still greatly interested in Marie's welfare, has managed to see her daughter and herself as being more distinct and hence has been able to establish a better relationship with her. She has made more friends and developed some new interests. She begins to miss the odd session again and one day says she would like to try to manage on her own for a bit. The counsellor suggests Pamela might fear becoming too dependent on their relationship but this tentative interpretation evokes no response from Pamela and the counsellor chooses not to pursue it. She feels a fair amount has been achieved; she is aware of more work that might be done around Pamela's struggles to balance her feelings about closeness and control in her intimate relationships but recognises Pamela's reluctance to engage further and respects her wish for autonomy. She encourages Pamela to come for a further six weeks so that they can have time together to reflect on the meaning of their work and the experience of ending. Pamela agrees and continues to say how grateful she is for the counselling and how much it has helped her through a difficult period. The counsellor finds the ending slightly unsatisfactory as she feels Pamela shies away from a deep exploration of loss and the meaning of her dependence on the counsellor. However, her knowledge of her client's history and the glimpses of the extent of her pain about being abandoned which Pamela has allowed at some points in the counselling mean that the counsellor does not persist too strongly in her comments about the significance of the loss. Recognising that Pamela is still fairly vulnerable, she leaves an open door saying she will see Pamela again if the need should arise.

Discussion

Some might question our prescription of long-term work for Pamela because of her apparently limited ability to tolerate psychological challenge and ambivalent motivation. One of our respondents writes:

> The people most suitable for long-term work tend to be people who have difficulties of a long-standing nature, and who want to address

these difficulties in order to make significant changes. Such people also must have the emotional and mental strength to 'endure' such work as it is usually very demanding. There would be no point offering long-term work to people who are in some sort of crisis and are only wanting to get some help to get through the crisis. I personally would not offer long-term work to a client who was not willing to look at the past's influence on the present, as I work from a psychodynamic point of view.

Elton Wilson also argues that 'longer-term psychological therapy is an option to be considered only by clients with enough stability and ego-strength to consider themselves as discerning customers' (1996: 176).

We would be less sure about this judgement while endorsing her approach of not necessarily offering long-term help in cases like Pamela's. It is true that Pamela could have been offered no more than support in the initial crisis and that this in itself might have been useful to her. One possible intervention would have been to offer repeated crisis help on demand and a more pressurised counsellor might have arranged that she and the GP share such support.

Short-term focused work does not seem an option to us: Pamela's vulnerability and low initial motivation exclude her from brief dynamic therapy according to one set of criteria (Malan and Osimo, 1992); her difficulty in tolerating loss according to another (Mann and Goldmann, 1994). She might have been deemed suitable for cognitive analytic therapy which does take on clients like Pamela whom it might describe as suffering from personality related problems and does claim some success with them (Ryle, 1990). We are not sure that Pamela would have been able to make the necessary commitment at the time of her first presentation. We think she falls into the category considered by Feltham as unsuitable for a short-term intervention:

> Those who are severely damaged and unsupported — it is relatively easy to identify who has deeply entrenched character problems, whose depression is severe, who has been exposed to multiple abuse and trauma. (Feltham, 1997: 52)

An immediate offer of long-term work would have alarmed Pamela. She would not have complained or asked for more if the counsellor had ended the work when Marie returned home. We think, however, that she would have either returned with the next crisis or possibly presented to the GP with repeated episodes of depression if her long-standing, deep distress had not been responded to. We feel an opportunity for Pamela to become a little stronger would have been missed if the counsellor had not offered to go on working with her.

In describing Pamela as someone who has had an extremely difficult history, growing up without a stable carer, and who has held herself together in adult life by centring everything around her daughter, we are thinking of the many vulnerable people who may approach or be referred to counsellors. They do need support, particularly if they lose the person or mechanism they have used to give coherence to their lives, but they need to be allowed to go at their own pace, to give up their defences if and when they can. It is the counsellor's job to recognise such clients' genuine fragility and offer ongoing work when they have begun to feel some benefit; it is important to be very aware of what clients can tolerate. Counsellors should try not to miss opportunities. There is a place for offering but not insisting on insight and transference interpretations as one might with someone more robust. Sometimes a lengthy period of supportive work may prepare the ground for more intense interpretative work later.

Klein, a psychotherapist, writes movingly about clients like Pamela and the danger of challenging and interpreting too early in the therapeutic relationship:

> Some people are so dominated by their pain that they cannot concentrate on much else . . . They need to complain to us until they are sure that we mind about their pain, before we can educate them into taking an interest in its unconscious meaning. People in pain cannot concentrate. (Klein, 1995: 99)

> We sometimes interpret defences without making sufficient allowance that what is being defended against is not an 'I' in the usual sense of the word. Pain is being defended against. But no clear inner object is being defended. If, then, we penetrate the defences, we have a patient on our hands who is defenceless against his or her unprocessed and now uncontainable feelings! Their ego was not strong enough to contain them! We have allowed them to be overwhelmed. (Klein, 1995: 109–10)

She argues that the initial work with this kind of client is in affirming them as human beings and helping clarify their feelings. It may take a long time for trust and the climate for making links between parts of a person's experience to be established. The practitioner must not rush such clients but concentrate on staying with and attending to them until some strength has developed.

In Pamela's case the counsellor's person-centred training helped her stay within her client's frame of reference. She was content to use her psychodynamic understanding to think about her client but she did not insist on Pamela's accepting an interpretative way of working. Pamela was not 'cured' but she was helped – more than she might have been by repeated crisis interventions, courses of medication and possible hospitalisation. It may be that the timely provision of long-term counselling in such cases even results in long-term savings for the NHS as well as in improved coping and peace of mind for the client. (See Tolley and Rowland, 1995, for a discussion of the evaluation of the cost effectiveness of counselling in healthcare.)

Joy White

Scene One

Joy is a 23-year-old woman with a part-time job in a library. For the last two years she has been finding everyday life very tiring; even the most simple household tasks seem an effort and although she likes her job she has been considering giving it up because she finds organising herself to get there on time very draining. A friend has suggested she try counselling and given her the phone number of a local voluntary counselling agency. Joy has been looking at the number for some days and has just summoned up the courage to dial.

She asks if she can make an appointment. The receptionist senses her nervousness and takes time to get and give the necessary information. She offers Joy an appointment in two weeks' time, explaining that this is what the agency calls an intake appointment for Joy and the counsellor to discuss what she needs; if they decide that ongoing counselling is indicated Joy will have to see another counsellor. She explains that the agency asks people to contribute towards their counselling according to their means but has a policy of not excluding those who can't afford to pay much. Joy can discuss this with the counsellor at the initial meeting. Joy is reassured by the receptionist's clarity and matter of factness and by her not asking why Joy wants counselling. She decides she will keep the appointment.

Scene Two: The intake interview

Joy is very nervous and has no idea how to begin. The counsellor asks her what has brought her. Joy describes how depressed she has been feeling, what an effort it is to get up in the morning, how she often retreats to the sofa with a box of chocolates for hours on end, how she feels 'in a fog' half the time. She can't offer any clear cause for feeling like this or connect the onset of these feelings with any particular event. The only possible reason she mentions is that she had gone on an Access course; many of the other students had proceeded to university but she had decided being a full time student would be too difficult and too expensive although she had done well on the course and felt it had helped her make up for the schooling she had missed in her early teens when she had hated the thought of school and stayed at home a great deal.

The counsellor asks about her relationships. Joy is rather embarrassed and gives a halting description. She became engaged when she was only 19, soon after she left home to live alone in a bedsit. Her relationship with her fiancé is 'OK, but not very exciting'. She thinks she would like a child sometime.

At first it seems she is going to have little to say about her childhood either – she says that most of it is a blank. She does have some warm memories of her mother's mother with whom she lived when she was very young; otherwise her descriptions of family relationships are flat. It emerges that Joy's father died when she was 3 years old; her mother remarried and Joy never really got on with her stepfather. She can't remember her father but can recall her fury at the arrival of the stepfather when she was five. The counsellor enquires about her mother's reaction to this rage; Joy thinks her mother laughed at her protests but the energy goes out of her voice and the story tails off. She volunteers that she is an only child but seldom visits her parental home.

She becomes more animated when asked about her memories of hating school. She describes being bullied by a male teacher when she was eleven and avoiding school as much as possible for the next few years. Both her mother and stepfather had jobs and did not pay much attention to the initial tentative enquiries from the school. When the issue came to a head Joy had been forced back into regular attendance but no one had asked why she had wanted to stay away so much or helped her resettle when she returned. The counsellor asks how she felt then. 'Just confused, unhappy, not interested in anything. Like I often feel now I suppose.'

This acknowledgement paves the way for a discussion about what Joy might hope to gain from counselling. The counsellor does not say how long she thinks counselling might continue but she does say that it seems Joy has been unhappy and without anyone close to talk to for a long time and so it might mean that counselling will take some time. It will be up to Joy to decide the pace she works at and what is talked about. Joy looks relieved and says she would like to continue. She has forgotten that she will have to see a different counsellor for the ongoing work and is disappointed when the intake counsellor reminds her. Nonetheless she agrees to start as soon as there is a vacancy and to rearrange her schedule at the library if necessary.

The intake counsellor who is an experienced practitioner with special training in assessment is left mulling over her thoughts about Joy. She has succeeded in gathering a fair amount of information about this young woman's predicament without formally structuring the interview. The counsellor is clear about Joy's reasons for coming and how long she has felt depressed. She has some history of Joy's family and sense of her current situation. She speculates about different aspects of Joy's story, especially her poor relationship with the stepfather, her lack of contact with her family, the significance of the bullying schoolteacher and the embarrassment about her engagement. She wonders if Joy might have been abused in some way but thinks she was right not to ask this rather nervous client outright, particularly as Joy will now have to see a different counsellor. While Joy is not psychologically sophisticated, she has been able to convey her situation to the counsellor and make some relationship with her. The counsellor is clear that her offer of ongoing open-ended counselling is an appropriate one: Joy's difficulties are long-standing; she is obviously uncertain in her relationships and seems to be underachieving at work. At the same time she is not so disturbed that she is unable to sustain everyday living or make meaningful contact with others. She finds relief in talking about her feelings and wants to continue.

Starting out
Joy's counselling goes on for about four years and tests both her and the counsellor. The initial phase goes quite well. The agency specialises in psychodynamic work and offers training as well as counselling. It assigns Joy an inexperienced but sensitive female counsellor supervised by the intake counsellor. After Joy's initial difficulties about being handed over are dealt with the pair settle into a good working relationship. Joy is vastly relieved to have someone to talk to and the intensity of her depression abates. Indeed she soon rediscovers her intelligence and capabilities; first she is offered promotion at work, then she decides to apply to university after all. She is extremely grateful to the counsellor who can do no wrong in her eyes. Left to her own devices the counsellor might bask in this but her supervisor reminds her of the dangers of idealisation and keeping good and bad feelings completely separate and lodged in different people. She suggests the fact that Joy's relationship with her fiancé remains tepid may be significant and worth investigating. Despite the counsellor's exploring the possible relevance to herself of any negative comment, Joy persists in expressing only positive feelings towards her.

A crisis
After about a year Joy makes a visit to a Well Woman clinic with a friend who has suggested they both take advantage of the opportunity for a check-up. When the doctor is taking a cervical smear Joy finds herself suddenly very distressed. She finds it very painful and wants to pull away. The doctor, who is in fact being very gentle, asks afterwards what was wrong. Joy begins to weep uncontrollably. She has had a sudden memory of being penetrated against her will when she was a child. She can't remember everything but has a strong physical recollection of being unable to move, feeling hurt and frightened. The doctor sits quietly, giving Joy time, thinking it best not to ask too many questions which Joy might find intrusive. Her unobtrusive, prompting silence is helpful to Joy who finds herself saying that she had watched a television documentary about sexual abuse the night before. It made her feel sick and she had switched it off. Very tentatively the doctor asks if she thinks she could have been abused. Joy is confused, 'Maybe, I don't know, I can't remember much

*about my childhood.' She tells the doctor about her coun-
selling and the doctor suggests she discuss what has happened
with the counsellor.*

*This event initiates the second phase of Joy's counselling
during which she recalls and recounts her very painful
experience of being abused by her stepfather for much of her
childhood until she was eleven. The memories are retrieved
very slowly at first as the experience is so difficult to know
about. Later Joy has quite terrifying flashbacks when details of
what has happened come suddenly and unbidden into her
mind in a very distressing and vivid way. One of her strongest
feelings is of betrayal as she believes that her mother has
chosen not to know about the abuse. She had taken a job
involving frequent night shifts and seemed deliberately to
misunderstand Joy's attempts to talk to her about the stepfather. The loved grandmother had moved to another town
and Joy had not been able to confide in her. At times Joy is
overwhelmed by guilt in the counselling. She is afraid that the
abuse has been her fault, that she has somehow invited or
taken pleasure in it. She comes to realise how the abuse has
affected many areas of her life. Her preoccupation with it has
interfered with her ability to concentrate at school and made
her extremely sensitive to the bullying teacher's sexual
innuendo. The distrust she has learned through the abuse
means it is still difficult for her to have sexual pleasure and
this in turn is affecting her relationship with her fiancé.*

*The counsellor is not totally surprised by learning about the
abuse; it helps make sense of Joy's depression. She is very
careful to move at Joy's pace during the months when these
memories are the focus of the counselling. She is impressed by
Joy's strength. Although she is overtaken by so much painful
feeling she is living a much more active life, has started at
university and made a new group of friends. Joy continues to
describe the counsellor as the best thing that has happened to
her until a visit to her grandmother and an unplanned break
because of the counsellor's sudden hospitalisation together
precipitate a new phase in the counselling.*

A change in the counselling relationship
*Joy tells her grandmother about the abuse and is brushed
aside. The grandmother tries to pass it off as 'nothing very*

much' and retreats from any contact with Joy's distress. Joy is devastated by this reaction and feels very let down by the counsellor's unavailability during the crisis. The counsellor acknowledges her pain at being failed twice but is very taken aback when Joy begins to distrust her. For the first time in two and a half years Joy misses some sessions, questions the fee arrangements and complains that the counsellor misunderstands her. She wonders aloud about seeing the university counsellor instead: 'People say she's very good and a real feminist, totally on the side of women.' During this period Joy becomes very contemptuous of her fiancé and considers leaving him.

The counsellor is upset by the change in her client. She had been so pleased with their progress together which has helped her as well as Joy to grow in confidence. The supervisor is less dismayed. She points out that one way Joy has coped is by seeing some people in her life as very good and others as very bad. Until now the counsellor has been all good; if Joy can tolerate more mixed feelings towards her and others she may come to be stronger. This helps the counsellor reflect on her own tendency to cling to an overpositive view of those she is attached to which she works on in her personal therapy. She feels less threatened by Joy's attacks and persists in talking with her about the difficulty and confusion of having mixed feelings for those we care about. Gradually Joy's hostility to the counsellor abates as she explores her rage and disappointment.

The work continues for another year. Joy does break off her engagement; she makes good progress with her degree. After some three and a half years she feels strong enough to manage on her own. She discusses this with the counsellor and they arrange a date to end six months in advance. The closing phase of the counselling sees some return of her original depression but is most characterised by sadness about the absence of any close family relationship and gratitude to the counsellor for her persistent attempts to understand.

Discussion

In presenting this case history we are arguing for the desirability of allowing for the emergence of memories, experiences and conflicts as counselling progresses and being ready to adapt accordingly. The assessing counsellor in this instance could not have been sure of the meaning of Joy's childhood amnesia, underachievement, depression and unsatisfactory relationship, but she could sense that something was seriously amiss and offer the opportunity for open-ended work. Joy's ready acceptance of the offer is an important indication that she shares this perception and is ready to co-operate with the counselling; it is some confirmation that long-term work is an appropriate approach.

Medication might have had some impact on Joy's symptoms and might have been necessary for a period along with the counselling but it would not have reached the underlying causes of her depression. Group treatment might have been appropriate for Joy at some point. Herman and Schatzow (1984) argue that time-limited group therapy may be effective with survivors of abuse. Hall et al. (1995) report a reduction in depressive symptoms and use of psychiatric hospital and primary care services in women attending once weekly group analytic therapy for six months. It is possible that Joy –who does have considerable ego strength as well as a history of trauma – might have improved within a cognitive analytic or brief dynamic therapy framework. Ryle writes:

> It is still, in my experience, difficult to know in advance which patients are likely to require longer treatment. . . . Even in individuals who have a major difficulty in accessing their underlying feelings and memories (for example, schizoid personalities, patients with marked childhood amnesias), or in those with highly developed resistant symptomatic behaviours (such as anorexia, and bulimia), an initial brief intervention can achieve significant change, although further therapy will be required in most cases. (Ryle, 1990: 148–9)

However, we would argue that the offer of long-term work for people who have been (or whom the assessor senses may have been) sexually abused or otherwise severely traumatised in childhood and who respond positively to such an offer is preferable; it allows time to work through the consequences of the early experience which are usually many and serious. For a fuller discussion of the issues involved in working with clients who have been sexually abused, see Walker (1992) who presents accounts of survivors in their own words as well as discussing the professional questions arising from this work.

We would argue that Joy needed to trust the counselling relationship before she could even recall the abuse. People like her, even when they present with abuse as the issue, need the opportunity to go at their own pace and to come to feel that they have some control of the process. Longer term work gives them the chance to explore their difficulties over trusting anyone else; to see what they may have internalised and be re-enacting of past abusive relationships, to mourn for a missed childhood and, if things go well, find a realistic courage to go on with their lives more creatively.

This kind of provision is most likely to allow for the emergence of and helpful work with negative transference which is why we have made it such an important part of Joy's progress in counselling. Joy's early idealisation of the counsellor was really a defence against the fear of losing or destroying anything good in her life; she needed time to risk integrating her positive and negative feelings. As Molnos points out:

> The patient whose damage is so early that he cannot tolerate his own emotional ambivalence when confronted with it needs to be held for a while before the split can be healed. In other words he needs a relatively longer therapy. (Molnos, 1995: 59)

Tom Cook

Scene One: A social work supervision session
between Tom and his male manager
Tom is a young man of 31 in his first professional job as a social worker. He is in trouble with his manager/team leader who considers Tom can never accept anything on trust but has to argue every issue, however trivial, in team meetings and supervision. To make matters worse he doesn't do the work assigned to him. He can spend ages with one client and completely neglect another. He is in danger of being subject to disciplinary proceedings but his tolerant manager has decided to raise the matter in supervision before moving to a more formal level. He outlines clearly and calmly his view of Tom's shortcomings and the likely consequences if he does not change. He suggests that some counselling help might be useful to Tom – he is tactful enough not to say 'with your problems about authority'. At the same time he makes it clear that Tom's behaviour cannot be tolerated any longer. Counselling is not to be seen as a soft option; he is suggesting it out of concern for Tom but his first responsibility is to the work of

the department and the social work clients. Tom is very taken aback and shocked to realise how much trouble he is in. He is also fleetingly impressed by his manager's directness. Somewhat sulkily he mutters that he will make an appointment to see the staff counsellor.

Scene Two: The first meetings
The counsellor explains that the social services department provides up to six sessions free for its employees under an employee assistance programme. Perhaps Tom can tell him why he has come. They can take this meeting and perhaps another to make some sense of the issues and see whether or not Tom wants to carry on with counselling.

Tom is not at all sure how much he wants to co-operate but he begins to describe his view of the work situation. He is interested in the work but doesn't see the point of 'all the bureaucracy'. He feels his manager is always trying to interfere and the others just go along with the agreed procedures for a quiet life; they don't care about the clients the way he does. The counsellor doesn't comment on this but instead asks Tom about his previous experience of work. Tom has done a number of unskilled jobs, none for very long. He tells how he would get fed up after a while and either find something that appeared more promising or have a spell of unemployment. He explains that his motivation to train as a social worker came from a period in a relationship with an older woman who encouraged Tom to make something of his life. He had left home early and been in various sorts of minor trouble before meeting her. The counsellor comments that the social work job seems to represent a real achievement for him; one it now seems he may sabotage. Tom agrees rather sulkily that he was pleased when he got the job but can't see how he might be undermining his own success.

The counsellor doesn't insist on his suggestion but asks for some information about Tom's family. He has come from a family of five boys and one girl who was the youngest and last child. Tom was the last of the boys to be born. His mother had been ill for much of his childhood and had died when he was thirteen. His father and all the brothers had competed for her attention but there was never enough to go round and she was happiest with her only daughter. There had not been much love lost between the men of the family; Tom had been bullied by his brothers. After his mother's death there had been little to keep him at home.

Tom tells this story with little evidence of concern for himself and little apparent expectation that he might evoke any response in the counsellor who is puzzled how to proceed. In his mind the counsellor makes links between Tom's early experience with his father and his current conflict with his male manager and between the older woman and the missing mother. In this the counsellor is much influenced by his own current psychodynamic therapy and his personal preoccupation there with issues of rivalry with his father for his mother's attention. However, at the moment he is more concerned to make emotional contact with Tom. He comments on how difficult it must have been for Tom to feel second best to his sister and not to have as much of his mother's attention as he would have liked. Briefly Tom looks very upset but then describes an occasion when he had had his mother all to himself on a trip to the woods and how wonderful that had been for both of them. Time is running out; the counsellor has information and some useful hypotheses but no contract and no clarity about a workable focus for the six sessions he can offer. He invites Tom to return the following week to see if they can together identify an area to work on in the time available. Tom says he supposes he has nothing to lose.

Tom is late for the next session and begins by asking if the counsellor has yet worked out how his experience as a baby has made him how he is he now. The counsellor doesn't rise to this provocation and, rather shamefacedly, Tom says he supposes they should talk about work. The counsellor agrees and suggests they look at Tom's relationship with his manager and any possible parallels there might be with his relationship with his father. Tom comments that he hasn't been near his father for three years and couldn't care less if he were dead but agrees to the focus: 'If you think that's right. After all, I suppose you're the boss.'

The ongoing work
This is hardly a promising beginning. Tom feels under pressure to use counselling, is not sure it will help and is

*protecting himself with a rather hostile passivity. Nonetheless
the counsellor perseveres over the next few sessions. He adopts
a gently confrontative approach, drawing a number of
parallels between Tom's reaction to him and his manager and
occasionally pulling in references to the past as well. Tom
responds a bit and seems to be in less trouble with the team. In
the sixth session the tone is rather different. Tom speaks in a
much more feeling way about his loneliness as a child, his
sense of being the wrong sex – a disappointment and burden
to his parents. The rather inexperienced counsellor is
prompted by this to ask if Tom wants to continue counselling
and offers to see him privately for a reduced fee. (He is
engaged in further training and wants some experience of
long-term work.) Tom accepts hesitantly.*

*He uses some of the time to talk a little more about his
childhood, the important relationship with the older woman
and his pain at its ending. He continues to stay out of serious
trouble at work but on the whole the private counselling does
not go very well. Tom comes on and off for several months but
never becomes fully engaged in the process. The counsellor
has not taken any private clients before; he has to arrange to
rent a suitable room at short notice and therefore has little
choice of times to offer Tom, which becomes a bone of con-
tention between them. The counsellor is embarrassed at
charging even a reduced fee and Tom is resentful about
paying at all, especially for missed sessions. The counsellor's
supervisor has suggested that the counsellor be less focused in
his interventions now that the arrangement is open-ended but
Tom does not respond well to this new approach and often
complains that he doesn't know what to talk about; he
enquires if he is supposed to be 'in touch with his inner child'
or denying a hidden attraction to the counsellor. Both counsellor and client become frustrated. The counsellor, who is
deeply involved in his own therapy and training, cannot
understand Tom's apparent lack of curiosity about himself.
Tom feels he is making no progress. He hasn't got a clear
purpose in mind but does know that he often feels depressed
and discontented and hopes that somehow counselling can
help; instead he is feeling he is a failure at counselling too. He
can't quite believe the counselling is really for him; there is of
course some little justification for this in the reality of the*

*counsellor's need for training which Tom doesn't know about
but senses. More important is the way his past experience of
not being wanted for himself, of having something done to
him, of not being an active agent in his own life, becomes
replayed in the counselling despite all the counsellor's conscientious efforts to help. Perhaps he is over-eager in his
interpretations; Tom certainly feels attacked on some occasions. Neither counsellor nor client can bring himself to name
and discuss the discomfort openly. Eventually Tom breaks off
counselling by simply stopping coming for sessions without
giving any notice or explanation for his absence. It is the
counsellor's turn to feel unwanted and a failure.*

Discussion

In this example we are suggesting that long-term work can drift on
in a rather unhelpful way. One of our respondents comments:

> Long-term clients where I afterwards have wished I hadn't offered it
> have tended to be when I felt over-optimistic about my own abilities,
> or got sucked into a (counter) transference reaction of wanting to help
> without properly analyzing it. Result: lots of time spent with little
> gained except the client being able to say that they've tried counselling
> and it didn't help.

It may be that the combination of Tom's reluctance and the
counsellor's misplaced zeal (evident in their failure to agree a clear
contract) led to the unsatisfactory conclusion. Tom might have
responded better to a more person-centred approach and almost
certainly to a counsellor with the confidence to name and explore
the lack of congruence between them more directly.

Tom does have many difficulties but he is not yet very motivated
to engage with them in long-term counselling. Unlike Pamela, who
welcomes her counsellor's invitation to more open-ended work
after an initial less committed period of counselling, or Joy who is
ready for the offer at once, Tom feels shamed by the suggestion
that he might need many sessions of counselling and frightened of
what he might reveal if he lets himself get further involved. The
fact that the original referral came from his manager increases his
fear. The counsellor makes the offer of ongoing work rather
impulsively, without sufficient assessment of Tom's history and

motivation and without discussion with his supervisor (which might well have included reference to the BAC Code of Ethics for Counsellors' stipulations about contracting and consideration of possible ethical issues involved in moving a client from an agency to a private setting). There is some evidence for Tom's lack of readiness to engage seriously with counselling – he comes at his manager's suggestion, not under duress but certainly because he is in trouble. His attitude to the counsellor and his own feelings is sometimes flippant; he covers his discomfort with a rather passive–aggressive stance.

We would suggest that this counsellor might have been better to stick to the original agreement about meeting six times and to have concentrated on the work issues. Here he is right to focus on the rivalry Tom undoubtedly feels with other men. But there are clearly much deeper seated and more complex problems which the counsellor understands much less clearly. He might have responded to the greater depth of feeling in the last of the six sessions by acknowledging Tom's difficulty in ending and his gratitude for being taken seriously. He could have suggested that Tom think about whether or not he wanted counselling in the future but left it to him to ask and make the arrangements himself. Instead the counsellor – influenced partly by his own need for training clients and let down by an inadequate grasp of his client's difficulties – allowed himself to be drawn into an unhelpful battle about who wanted whom.

It is not that Tom did not have serious issues to address: he was burdened not only with his problems with authority but also with a much deeper seated disturbance in his sense of his own self-worth. However, at this time he was not yet ready to acknowledge this, probably because he could sense both the counsellor's lack of confidence and how painful exploring further might be. It is just possible that a more experienced and less anxious counsellor might have succeeded in engaging Tom or at least in confronting the difficulties and helping him to make a proper ending which might have made it easier for him to return to counselling in the future. We are not suggesting that people in training should not undertake long-term work, although a private setting is not one we would recommend; we are saying that their clients need to be carefully selected and have some motivation for change. The enthusiasm of the new counsellor may certainly be useful in helping generate hope in clients but it can also blind the counsellor to clients' ambivalence and a more distanced perspective on the dynamics of the counselling.

David Da Silva

Scene One

It is a busy Friday afternoon in the university counselling service, three weeks into the autumn term. The counsellor is waiting to see a new client who is late. The receptionist has informed her that the student had telephoned three weeks ago to make an appointment but then had telephoned a week later to rearrange it for the current time. The numbers of students attending the service have been growing rapidly in size after a slow start to the term's work and the counsellor is beginning to think about whether the service should soon be re-establishing a waiting list and whether the team ought to reconsider the manner in which it is put into practice. The counsellor also begins to ponder about the student's lateness when he arrives.

David apologises for his lateness. He is a young man of 20 years with long unkempt hair who is dressed in jeans and T-shirt. He explains that he had been to see the dentist before counselling and there had been a much longer wait than he anticipated. He is slightly built and tall with a charming smile that makes him seem younger than his age. He is pleased to be able to see a counsellor because he found the help that he received in hospital was 'great' – they mainly just talked to him about his feelings and he felt they really understood him. He had been going back as an outpatient for a while and knew that it was important to keep seeing someone. He really liked the junior doctor whom he had ended up seeing once a week and found that he was starting to view the world quite differently now. He peers at the counsellor over his spectacles and says, 'It's a bit funny to say it, I suppose, but ending up in hospital has done me a lot of good. I've learned a lot about myself. I was pleased that Dr O'Malley wanted me to see you.'

The counsellor asks him about why he has been in hospital and discovers that David had suffered a manic episode six months ago when he was in Spain on a geography field trip in the Sierra Nevada. He had stopped eating and drinking and had become convinced that people in the nearest village wanted him to live with them permanently. He spoke no Spanish. He had begun to believe that he could help them find a better source of water for their crops and that he needed to lead forays into the more remote parts of the Sierra to restore the aqueduct systems of the Moors. The other students had been angry with him for disappearing when project work needed completing together, but eventually both fellow students and tutors realised he was ill. They had to stop him trying to set off for a remote peak in the middle of the day when the sun was very hot. He had become aggressive and insisted he could climb the mountain alone.

David tells his colourful story with dignity. He realises that he was ill and cannot remember some details. He has been ill before when he was studying for his A-levels but that seemed to him to have been a question of exam anxiety. He was in hospital only very briefly at that time but had spent two months in hospital this year and had continued as an out-patient until his return to university. He is repeating his first year.

The counsellor listens to his story and is aware as David speaks that he gives a clear account of a confusing episode though she has little information yet about any precipitating factors, his life history or family background. She is also surprised to hear that the GP in student health has informally referred David without discussing the referral. She suggests that it might be helpful if she could, with his permission, talk to Dr O'Malley. David thinks it would be very helpful and that he would mention it to him on Monday, when he next intends to see him. The counsellor wonders, privately, if she should accept this arrangement. She makes an appointment for David for the following Friday and suggests that if the GP hasn't phoned by then she will contact him. David agrees. As she sees him to the door, he turns and says, 'I'm sorry I was late. Thank you very much for seeing me.' He hesitates and smiles, 'I'll be here on Friday then.' He still lingers and the counsellor says purposefully, 'Yes. I will see you on Friday, then.'

Scene Two
On the next Friday the counsellor is waiting to see David who is not yet late. She has spoken to the GP who did indeed

*telephone after seeing David. He told her that he had tried
several times to speak to her before she saw David but had not
left a message. He is seeing David regularly to monitor his
lithium levels. David had been diagnosed as manic-depressive
by the psychiatrist in his home town who had treated him in
hospital. The prophylactic treatment of lithium took some time
to establish in terms of optimum dosage. He would be very
grateful if she would let him know how she found David and
whether or not she would be able to continue to see him. The
GP thought he was 'a nice lad' and that it was possible that he
might be OK given some support, though he had wondered if
it was a little early to come back to university.*

*As she waits, the counsellor wonders about the meaning of
David's reluctance to leave the previous week. She is also
aware of feeling quite cautious about seeing him while at the
same time entertaining quite positive reactions to him – his
account of his breakdown was very moving, as was his
emotional simplicity in the telling of it.*

*David arrives on time. He tells her about his academic
work and how worried he is about keeping up. Last year had
been something of a disaster. He had already changed course
from the previous year because he didn't like it at all. He had
left and come back the following year to start again on the
new course but had not settled into work and then there had
been the business in Spain. He is also worried about where he
is living and wants to move. The counsellor listens and tries to
understand, though many thoughts are in her mind about
why his student career is proving to be so long drawn out,
what kind of family dynamics he may be caught up in and
whether or not he is seeking help to think about all these issues
and their relationship to his breakdown. She suggests that
there seems to be a lot to talk about and that perhaps they
should arrange to meet for the rest of term and then decide
whether or not to carry on after Christmas. David is a little
surprised and tells the counsellor that he knows it will help
him and he would like to carry on with counselling. The
counsellor also makes a link between the pressures he had to
deal with in his previous year at university and the episode in
Spain and works out with David what they can agree should
happen if 'stress' starts seriously to affect his health. He is very
keen to keep the GP informed if he or the counsellor start to*

worry that his health might suffer. He is confident in both the counsellor and the doctor and has no qualms in agreeing to their communicating about him.

Scene Three
At David's third meeting with the counsellor, he is extremely worried about where he is living and is making plans to move out into a bedsit on his own. He doesn't like the other students he lives with and has heard about a flat on the edge of town. He is also planning to stand as secretary of the music society. The bedsit would be closer to the rehearsal rooms. He has become friendly with an older man in the society, though he hasn't told him yet about his plans to try and oust the current secretary. While the counsellor gently encourages David to talk and think about what would be best for him, she is aware of a growing anxiety that he is becoming 'high'. She tells him that it all sounds exhausting, especially when he has so many other considerations to keep in mind. He says he has not been sleeping very well but that he has made sure that he keeps eating and drinking properly because that was how it all started in Spain. The counsellor wonders aloud if David has thought what would it would be like if he were to move into the bedsit, as it is so far removed from the student area of town. He is concerned he could get a bit isolated in the flat. By the end of the session David is speaking more calmly about both the move and the possibility of taking more responsibility in the music society. He is due to see his GP the next week and the counsellor suggests that he tell him that he is sleeping badly.

Scene Four
The counsellor and David are meeting in the week before the university breaks up for the Christmas vacation. David is calm and fairly settled. He is cancelling the next session but wants to meet after Christmas. The series of counselling sessions has helped David work through the tension and stresses involved in returning to university without him becoming ill. He has been seen every week by the GP and by the counsellor. He has also formed a close relationship with the older man from the music society who is married and has

*offered David lodgings in his home. The counsellor feels the
transition back to university has been successful and that
David has avoided another crisis. Although she is psychodynamic in her outlook she has not used transference
interpretations with her client, sensing that this would take
him into a realm of relational issues which would be too
arousing emotionally for him at the moment. Nevertheless, she
is aware that he seems to look upon her as a kindly parental
figure and that the Christmas break may be difficult for him
in various ways. It has become clear over time that David's
father has his own problems and is obsessed with work and
his status as a leading figure in the world of the arts. David's
mother is not a clear figure in the counsellor's mind – she
appears as benign but ineffectual.*

*David is rather subdued in the session. He describes how he
will spend the break. He will be working to earn some money
and will not see many friends. He has few friends at home
because he was seen as rather 'swotty' when he was younger
and his crisis over the A-levels convinced local schoolfriends
that he was 'weird'. He speaks without enthusiasm but
professes to be really pleased to be going home to see his
family. He has also become much more involved in a choir
over the last term and will miss his friends. The counsellor
does not make an interpretation but acknowledges how
Christmas can be such a complex mix of good and bad
things. She clarifies that she will be there when he gets back
and they can decide whether or not he would like to carry on
meeting regularly. She also gives him the counselling service
phone number in case he needs to contact her at all while he
is away. She gently surveys and sums up the work they have
done together to help him make a successful adjustment back
into university.*

*The next week the counsellor receives a phonecall from
David's father thanking her for the help given to his son and
expressing the fear that he had gone back to university 'too
soon'. He feels that the psychiatrist had been too eager to
diagnose David as suffering from 'bi-polar affective disorder':
'He's always been so good at school, I think the exams got him
down at A-level and he's never quite recovered his confidence.
Do you think that I am handling him the right way? Is it
alright if I phone you later this week?'*

Scene Five
After the break David returns to counselling and decides he would like to see the counsellor every week until the end of the academic year. He wants to make sure that he stays in a good frame of mind so that he can get past the first year of the degree. He has been thinking about the period in Spain and he doesn't really understand what it all meant. 'Do you think that I will be able to understand it or should I just get on and put it behind me and forget about it?' The counsellor is posed with a direct question and she has to think about what kind of answer would be helpful and honest. She says plainly that she doesn't know, but perhaps the two of them can talk about what he thinks and see if they can make sense of it together. She adds, cautiously, that sometimes the meaning of experiences does not become apparent for a long time and that it is important to try to get on with your life whether you understand it or not.

Ongoing work
The contract to work together, with a remit to look beyond the immediate issues of reading for a degree was made in a tentative way. The counsellor telephoned the GP and told him that she had contracted to meet together with her client for the rest of the year but that she wanted to work with David in a way which did not disturb his equilibrium too much. The GP, who had worked with the counsellor in a collaborative way with other students, was pleased to make himself available if she should need to consult with him over David. He had stopped seeing David so regularly and now planned to see him once a term except for emergencies of any kind. Subsequently, David made some efforts to talk about his experiences at a deeper level than hitherto but found 'when I feel like I'm just going to open the trapdoor and see what's there, it goes all dark'. This poignant expression marked a turn away from 'understanding' to 'getting on' when David spoke mainly about his day-to-day concerns. He was able to talk about his family and the difficulties he felt he had with his father but said very little about his mother. He was afraid he might not possess his father's artistic talents. The counsellor did not feel it was appropriate to try to push open the trapdoor that David described by the use of

interpretations because she did not think that he would be able to survive the emotional experience without breaking down.

David's counselling over the next two terms was complicated by another hypomanic crisis and his involvement in an animal rights group. This time the counsellor had to involve the GP when David turned up, unexpectedly, at her office in a dishevelled state and talking incessantly. He was able to recognise, with the help of the counsellor and supported by his older friend, that the signs of a crisis were present and that medical help was needed. A short stay in a local clinic was arranged and David, who surreptitiously had been trying to wean himself off his medication, soon settled back into student life. The crisis was brought about after David had fallen in love with one of the girls in the group and was beginning to talk about wanting to have a relationship with her. He was clearly entertaining sexual feelings for her.

The period after this crisis was a difficult one for the counsellor who found David less and less accessible in the sessions. He did not seem to be disturbed but rather distracted. His plans to have a girlfriend had fallen apart and he seemed bored and uninterested in his life. He was not able to think about the connection between his wanting to be loved by the girl and her lack of interest in him with his low mood. He passed his exams at the end of the year, however, and again had managed to secure himself some paid work over the summer at home. Though lacking in the excitement which had sometimes marked his earlier mood, he managed to maintain a student life which involved his work, his music and membership of the animal rights group.

At one point, however, the older friend with whom he lodged asked David to ask if the counsellor could speak to him. The counsellor discussed this with David who wanted her to speak to his friend but who did not seem to know why it would be a good idea. When the meeting was arranged, the friend told the counsellor that he thought it was time David stopped counselling and that the animal rights group, of which he too was a part, would take care of David. The friend was suspicious of 'establishment do-gooders'. He explained that David had been 'screwed up by the system' and needed to be looked after by people on the same wavelength. The counsellor heard the friend out and simply said that it was up to David to decide what kind of help he wanted.

After the summer break David returned to see the counsellor. He had met some new friends on his temporary job over the summer and was planning to visit them soon. He was very keen on one girl whom he was hoping to court – he had acquired a radical haircut and new clothes. Moreover, there had been a marked change in the family situation. David's father had been to see a psychologist who was helping him to cope better with stress. Summer had been boring but uneventful until the girls started at work. He wondered if he could see the counsellor, but not every week, this term to make sure everything was OK. The counsellor agreed to see David fortnightly for the rest of term.

Ending

Over the last period of David's counselling he was again unable to explore his feelings and thoughts very far but now seemed less inclined to anyway. He had started up a relationship with one of the girls and would go over to visit or she would visit him. He now lived in a student house where there were no members of the animal rights group. He was struggling with his work which he was able to say was a lot harder than he'd ever thought a degree would be. He thought he was probably not as clever as his father but that it did not seem to matter much to anyone else but himself. The counsellor found the work with David a little dull at times – he seemed to have become 'just another student'. She still liked him and was pleased to see him but began to think she had outgrown her usefulness. The counselling did not end formally. David began to miss sessions and eventually stopped attending. The counsellor wrote saying that she thought he might have wanted to stop seeing her and that if this was the case it was fine by her but to get back in touch if he wished to see her in the future. There was no reply. She let the GP know that she had not seen David for some time at the end of the first term. He had seen David only once recently and that was in connection with a minor medical problem. This probably meant that David was well and happy but the counsellor will never know because she never saw him again.

Discussion

The counsellor's work with David will be discussed further in Chapter 4 on assessment and Chapter 5 on managing the work, in particular. It is an example of what we might describe as supportive long-term counselling and what Holmes calls 'supportive psychotherapy' which he points out is something of a misnomer:

> First, that there is no such unique thing as supportive psychotherapy: what this account attempts to describe is just psychotherapy practised with difficult patients in a low-key way. Second, that there is no such thing as unsupportive therapy: all therapy is, or should be, supportive. Psychotherapy is, among other things, about being nice to people – not in the sense of pandering, but by attending to them and taking them seriously. (Holmes, 1993: 58)

Holmes suggests that there are three categories of people who benefit from supportive psychotherapy (despite questioning its usefulness as a term):

- the psychologically disturbed patient;
- psychotherapists themselves who risk becoming engulfed in the clinical material with which they work;
- those people who work with disturbed patients, not delivering formal psychotherapy or counselling but who are involved with them as social workers, nurses, GPs and so on.

Whether or not all of Holmes' three categories of client would benefit from supportive as opposed to other forms of psychotherapy is contentious and perhaps a trifle confusing since they will all differ in their emotional and psychological capacities. However, the need for the long-term support of counselling is quite clear where people have suffered major psychological disturbance.

David's example is not uncommon in student counselling centres and may represent a particularly fortunate disturbed person since he was young and academically able by most standards. He was also able to support himself financially for brief periods and could rely on a comfortably well-off family at other times. The principles of helping someone similar to David would not alter if circumstances were more adverse though the management of the case may be focused on other issues.

Holmes suggests that supportive analytic psychotherapy greatly depends on positive transference:

> The therapist catches a glimpse of hope despite the difficulties the patient presents. The patient senses this appreciation of his specialness and responds positively. These positive feelings of the patient for the therapist must not be mistaken for reality, but should be interpreted only with extreme caution. It is often a relief when negative transference finally surfaces. (Holmes, 1993: 61)

David's positive transference to his counsellor started before he arrived at her door – he had liked his junior doctor and his GP and was anticipating that the counsellor would be helpful.

Holmes' account of the requirement to rely predominantly on 'non-specific factors' (Stiles et al., 1986), such as the personal qualities of the counsellor to create a trusting and reliable relationship where the client will be accepted and attended to with care and respect, is synonymous with the skills and qualities that good counsellors of all orientations possess. There is nothing particularly 'analytic' in his description apart from the concept of transference and the question of whether or not the counselling relationship is 'real', but these are conceptual issues not performative ones. He does introduce a notion of 'containment' which is important.

This analytic concept is a metaphorical reference to the earliest relation we all have had to our first caregivers. A mother who could not act like a protective shield around her baby until the baby is developed enough to contain its own feelings and experiences would be a poor container. Similarly, counsellors and therapists who work with very disturbed clients or patients may need to be able to contain feelings and thoughts for the clients until they can hold them and psychologically process them. David's counsellor is aware of his difficulties as someone who has been diagnosed as suffering from an affective disorder, but she also relates to him as a returning student with a lot of practical matters to sort out. The focus she offers David in the first 'trial' period of counselling and later when he is struggling academically demonstrates how even in long-term counselling there is a texture and shape to the work: it is not unfocused.

When David has made the transition back into the student life she gives him the opportunity to think about the experience he has been through but he cannot 'open the trapdoor' and she declines

to help force it open. Exploratory work with people who have
suffered psychotic breakdowns is beyond the remit of most
counsellors and psychotherapists. Many psychoanalysts would
also avoid entering this terrain though some psychiatrically
qualified analysts have shown that it is possible (for example,
see Rosenfeld, 1965). Such interventions will often require periods
of inpatient treatment. Instead, the counsellor stays at the level of
emotionality that seems to be optimal to the client's well-being.

Containment has a practical outcome which Holmes describes:

> The therapist sees himself as part of, and helps to create if necessary, a
> containing and supportive network for the patient: he must be
> prepared to collaborate with the patient's GP, social worker, priests or
> friends if necessary. The patient must be aware of this collaboration
> and inter-communication. This provides support for the therapist as
> well as the patient who may unconsciously wish to seduce the ther-
> apist into thinking that only he or she can help. The symbolic message
> to the patient that he is supported by a 'combined parent' . . . is
> important as a defence against destructive and splitting tendencies and
> also because the patient may often have lacked united parental
> support in childhood. (Holmes, 1993: 60)

David was lucky to have encountered a doctor and a counsellor
who had a good working relationship for each to take responsibility for managing the care of the client in their own way and to
communicate without a great deal of formality or conflict. Such
transactions are not always so amicable. As we know from David's
counselling, his experience of parents being able to work together
over difficult family problems was not extensive.

Counsellors may dispute some of the thinking behind Holmes'
view of containment or wish to think through on an ethical basis
how to ensure 'collaboration and inter-communication' does not
mean betraying trust or infantilising a client. However, many
counsellors will recognise that the skills involved in the work of
'the unsung craft' (Holmes, 1993: 67) of supportive psychotherapy
which has often been left by default to psychiatric services, are
commonplace among good counsellors in a range of less stigma-
tised services. Indeed, we would argue that, provided counsellors
are trained to work with people with serious psychological disorders and have the support of and access to psychiatrists and GPs
and that the agency in which they work can manage this kind of
work, they are likely to have an aptitude for this desperately
needed help.

Julia Roy

Scene One

It is very early in the morning at a large and prestigious hotel on the South Coast. Julia has walked the four miles in to work from her lodgings. She feels weak but tells herself to carry on walking up the steps to the foyer as briskly as she can. At the top she faints. Julia's supervisor has been worried for some time about the 17-year-old young woman who is working at the hotel as a trainee chef. Julia always looks tired and doesn't seem quite to fit in with the rest of the staff though she seems polite and pleasant. The supervisor has known another young woman who looked as thin as Julia and she was anorexic. The supervisor insists that Julia should sit down for a while in the staffroom and makes her a cup of tea. She tells Julia that she looks exhausted and seems a bit sad. Julia looks away – she has never liked to be singled out in any way and says she thinks she has the flu or something. The supervisor suggests she take some time off work and go to see her doctor. Julia agrees readily but something about her closed look makes the supervisor want to go further. She tells Julia about a previous colleague who found that she kept losing weight and avoided getting some help to keep herself healthy. Eventually, the girl had had to give up work and then became very depressed. She comments that Julia looks as if she is losing weight and maybe she is getting depression too? Julia hates the way the supervisor looks at her and stands up saying she is fine. The supervisor feels embarrassed that she has offended her and tells her that she can take a few days off but that the hotel won't be able to keep her on unless she is well enough to cope with the strenuous work in the kitchens.

Scene Two

A month later at the beginning of June, Julia is sitting in the interview room of a women's counselling service. She has asked to see a counsellor because she is afraid that if she does not get some help soon she is going to lose her job at the hotel. The counsellor is asking her what are her reasons for seeking help and Julia is trying to explain that she wants to see someone for advice only and that she has not got any real problems. The counsellor is curious and

*invites Julia to tell her the problem she needs advice about.
Julia explains that she used to be heavier than she is now
but decided to lose some weight and has reduced her size a
little bit. She is no longer losing weight but feels rather upset
that people at work might try to get rid of her because they
think there's something wrong with her. She tells the counsellor that she has a healthy appetite and that she eats well.
The counsellor helps Julia to begin talking about herself and
what it is that makes her feel so unconfident about her
future at work.*

*Julia starts to warm to the counsellor and speaks enthusi-
astically about her career plans and her love for the work that
she does. She begins to relax and to enjoy talking but becomes
very anxious when the counsellor asks her how much weight
she has lost and since when. It is difficult to follow the
account that Julia gives but something is said about her
mother remarrying which remains in the counsellor's mind.
At the end of the session the counsellor realises that Julia has
steered away from discussion of her eating and her weight
and has mainly talked about work. The counsellor knows
little about Julia's family background but is starting to put
together in her mind a picture of a young woman, living
away from home, who seems to be lacking confidence in
herself and her relationships with others. She suggests to Julia
that they could meet for a few sessions to discuss her problems
and that she can help her decide for herself how best to
manage things rather than tell her what she should do. Julia
looks pleased and makes another appointment.*

*The counsellor wonders whether or not Julia will turn up
the next time. She is intrigued by Julia who, when relaxed,
seems charming. She is rather surprised to see a client of
mixed race who has an eating disorder because she had
understood that this was a rare occurrence. However, she is
open-minded about such matters. The women's centre has
discovered that since appointing two black counsellors they
have attracted more black clients. The counsellor wonders if
Julia knows she could have asked to see a black worker.*

Scene Three
*Julia has been seen four times by the counsellor. She has
acknowledged that she had been continuing to diet when she*

first approached the service but has decided to call a halt to it as she has been getting so tired. She is hoping to keep her weight very low and is afraid that, despite reassurance from the counsellor, she will be encouraged to put on weight. She wonders if the counsellor has an eating disorder and secretly hopes she will not get as big as her. After the second session with the counsellor, Julia agreed to see her GP who examined her and agreed that she was anorexic but that she was not at a dangerous level of weight for her height. She offered to refer Julia to a specialist clinic at the local hospital but Julia said she would prefer to talk to the counsellor. The counsellor has telephoned the GP to confirm that she has taken Julia into counselling with her. The GP is rather sceptical about counselling and suggests that if Julia gets worse then she will have to refer her to the clinic, though there is a long waiting list. This is not the first time that the counsellor has seen someone with an eating disorder and she feels rather insulted. She swallows her pride and agrees that such a course of action might be appropriate if Julia were to get into further difficulties. The counsellor has always followed a policy of keeping in touch with a client's GP for clients like Julia but today she is wondering if it is worth it.

In this session the counsellor is clarifying with the client about when she is going to be away over the summer. The counsellor's holiday is booked for the whole of August and she is aware of what a big gap this will mean for Julia. They have several meetings booked before that time but Julia is taken aback at the length of the break. She does not express any concern about her well-being but does talk at length about what she has been eating. She has put on a small amount of weight (2lbs) and feels her weight is spiralling out of control. She is dreading the summer weather when everyone else will be wearing less clothing and will expect her to do the same. It gets very hot in the kitchen but she still tries to keep herself covered up as best as she can. Her father is expecting to visit with his new wife over the summer and she is dreading the meeting and sure she will not like his new partner. They will expect her to go out for meals with them and to the beach. As well as listening to the fears that Julia is expressing, the counsellor has also recognised that she is feeling that she will be very alone over the summer and that there will be many pressures on her which she is afraid she will not manage. She makes a tentative link between these factors and suggests that perhaps Julia is feeling the counsellor is going to be off on holiday just at a time when she needs her most and that this makes her feel very frustrated. This tentative transference interpretation is met with a blank look. 'Oh, no! I don't feel frustrated. You are entitled to go on holiday. Where are you going?'

Despite this response, the counsellor notices that Julia has started to look at her as she is speaking and later Julia goes on to say: 'It's funny when you say things like that – you're not angry when you say those sort of things, are you? I don't feel frustrated though I suppose I am a bit worried.'

Ongoing work
Julia continues to see the counsellor over the next year on a weekly basis. During this time she maintains a low weight, only slightly higher than the one she arrived with, and starts to have periods again. During the counselling Julia has been a 'model' client and has never needed any support in the breaks. She always shies away from any transference inter- pretations at first and will only take them in very gradually. She is particularly relieved when the counsellor mentions that she might feel worried about being expected to see the coun- sellor as the ideal weight. She has talked about her family and about her experience of being the only black child for many miles around in the village where she was born and lived with her mother. She hadn't thought of herself as black until she moved to the South Coast and went to work in the hotel which was quite multiracial. Here she felt very uncomfortable about her size. There were many other issues in Julia's life which she explored, especially as they linked into her use of food and starving to moderate her feelings.

Ending
As Julia gained in self-confidence she began to socialise with one of the other trainees from work and eventually started to see a boyfriend. Both she and her boyfriend decided they wanted to work in a more well-known London restaurant. The boyfriend managed to get a job there, soon to be followed

*by Julia. The counselling ended at that point. Julia was still
very preoccupied with keeping slim and liked to swim most
days but she was also very interested in her work and her
boyfriend. She sent the counsellor postcards from time to time
and after a year these stopped.*

Discussion

Eating disorders vary enormously in seriousness, from brief teen-
age problems to lifelong strugggles and from commonly held
attitudes (see Hsu, 1990) to peculiarly perverse relations to food
and eating (see Segal, 1993). Some clinicians follow treatment
schedules which attempt to cure the patient in a limited number of
sessions (see Crisp, 1965) and which report successful outcomes. It
is possible that someone like Julia may have been a suitable
candidate for such a programme, though she was not willing to
undertake a referral to a hospital in the first place and initially felt
reluctant to recognise the extent of her problem. Julia's counsellor
is able to help Julia with a major part of the difficulty in anorexia
which is the denial that the client is anorexic and that she would
like to avoid giving up self-starvation as a means of mediating her
relation to her self and others. Julia's loneliness and emotional
fragility go hand in hand with tenacious determination and will-
power. Such aspects of personality are not immediately apparent
in many anorexics when they present for counselling. In Julia's
case she encounters a counsellor who has experience of how these
factors can affect the counselling relationship and be expressed in
a compliant attitude which covers deep resistance to and fear of
change and loss of control. This knowledge enables the counsellor
to be able to contemplate the limits of her own competence and to
liaise with the GP and negotiate the outcome of such a consultation
should the client be referred elsewhere. The counsellor's ability to
be flexible over this matter may have helped the client to be able to
think realistically about her eating pattern. Although Julia does not
alter dramatically in terms of weight, she manages to give herself
enough to eat to remain at a non-threatening weight level and
begins to be able to express her concerns in dialogue with her
counsellor.

Lawrence writes encouragingly of her experience of working
with anorexic clients who may respond well to the kind of counselling approach taken here: 'The initial task is to enable the client

to share her own perceptions of her life, however confused and unclear these may be. It is important to remember that this may be the woman's first opportunity to attempt such a thing' (1984: 94). Lawrence also points out that the commitment a counsellor needs to make to enable the anorexic's process of self-discovery and to complete the 'task of translating the symptoms of anorexia into the realities and details of everyday life' (1984: 100) is significant and may take from one to four years (1984: 106).

Julia's sense of herself and feeling of racial identity are closely related to each other. Her counsellor is white, like all the other counsellors in this book and like the majority of counsellors in Britain. Julia may have preferred to see a black counsellor but she is not informed of this option. The counsellor senses that she may give the impression that she thinks race is an important factor before it has been identified as such. The issue of racial 'matching' in counselling is contentious and can be construed as exclusionary and collusive with white counsellor prejudice (see Littlewood and Lipsedge, 1989). The counsellor is also acutely aware of the need not to give any hint of rejection to a vulnerable client who already expresses fears of being persecuted by some-one at work who was apparently trying to be helpful. Although the question of how counsellors and clients from different ethnic groups may be affected by racial difference is beyond the scope of this book, racial difference may have played a part in the slowness of racial identity emerging as an important formative factor in Julia's understanding of herself. What is more clear is that time was certainly needed for Julia to find ways of making sense of her childhood experiences and their relation to the present. It may be that a black counsellor could have helped Julia more easily and in a shorter time, though there is no way of knowing this for sure.

More often than not clients are faced with the difficulty of finding any counsellor who is genuinely able to help rather than the best 'fit' although client–counsellor 'matching' has been researched and correlated with successful outcome. The concept of 'matching' is in general also related to long-term counselling. By temperament many counsellors prefer to work without the pressures of limited numbers of sessions and the same may be true for some clients, especially those who have felt emotionally deprived and for whom counselling becomes a taste of something that has long been hungered after.

May Maunders

Scene One

The counsellor has been allocated a new client in the bereavement counselling agency where he works as a volunteer one night a week. He has understood from Derek, a professional colleague who has done some limited counselling training with him in the past, that the client is a recently widowed young woman who has been causing concern at work. Derek has provided May with informal support at work but feels that his experience on the introductory course in counselling has not equipped him to carry on any further. He feels that after six months May should be much better than she is. Derek rang the agency to make the referral and spoke to the counsellor who asked him to get May to make an appointment.

The counsellor is rather disappointed that he has ended up being the one who will see May because he suspects that Derek is over-zealous in promoting bereavement counselling and wonders if he has inadvertently fostered this attitude in him on the course. He knows Derek will not pry into the counselling arrangements and that he is a kindly man but he feels uncomfortable all the same. As he waits for her to arrive he reads through the notes that he made when the call came through and wonders if he should acknowledge to Derek that May has made contact or not.

Scene Two

The counsellor goes to the reception to collect his new client. May is sitting in the drab waiting-room looking incongruously youthful and lively alongside the other two clients: an elderly man in dark clothes and a middle-aged woman in a raincoat who looks dejectedly at her feet. May smiles up at him pleasantly through her long blonde hair. She seems much younger than her 28 years and is dressed in fashionable sports clothes, looking as if she is about to set off for the gym. The counsellor is surprised as Derek gave him the impression that May had been tragically bereaved of her young husband and was not coping very well on her own.

Scene Three
*May tells her counsellor that she thinks she is OK, but having
spoken to Derek, she thought that it would be a good idea to
talk to someone who knows about all these things to check
that she was doing all she could to manage her affairs
properly now that she was on her own. She goes on to explain
that she had never had to do this before as she had lived with
her parents until she was 18 and had then married Joey and
moved into his house. He had organised everything for them
and was very keen on making sure they had good insurance
cover and savings plans. She looks sad for a short moment
and then asks the counsellor if he thinks she should spend any
of the money that has come to her. She then pauses and says
she assumed that Derek had told him about her husband. The
counsellor takes the opportunity to say that Derek has told
him that her husband was killed in a skiing accident six
months ago but that he doesn't know much else about what
has happened or about her.*

*May tells him in a calm factual way that her husband was
killed in a freak accident on the eve of their wedding
anniversary when they had been skiing in France and were
returning to their hotel. He had simply slipped but had injured
his head on concrete and died later in hospital. The counsellor
feels overwhelmed with sadness but May does not cry; indeed
it is as if she had rehearsed the description of the death. With
some difficulty, after having tried to respond empathically, the
counsellor prompts May to give him a picture of her present
situation. This is a little easier and May begins to talk more
freely and the counsellor is able to follow and reflect other less
extreme feelings and thoughts about all the new responsibilities she is struggling to manage. By the end of the session he
feels he is beginning to establish a rapport with her although
he is aware of thinking he must be careful not to put pressure
on her to talk about her feelings prematurely. When she has
gone he writes down a few notes for himself and realises that
in many ways it is as if he has just been talking with a
precocious child rather than an adult woman.*

Scene Four
*Six sessions later, May is telling the counsellor about some of
the problems she is facing at work. She returned after an*

absence of four months because her mother-in-law thought it would be good for her. However, she is unhappy because of the changed nature of her job. In her absence on compassionate leave her duties had been taken over by a new member of staff and she had been relegated to some basic jobs around the laboratories where she worked. The manager had done this originally so that if she wanted to go home at any point she could do so without worrying. May was angry about some criticisms of her work and wondered if she should give up altogether. Joey's death had meant that she had now acquired a considerable amount of money and could afford to take some time out. She also talks about how she might get an interior designer to redesign the house and that other people told her this would be a good idea. She might also buy a car and learn to drive.

The counsellor tries to follow May's words and to relate to the feelings behind them. He finds himself accompanying her on a circuitous ramble across many issues and many options. He has still not seen her cry but has been able to establish a safe environment and relationship where, so far, she has been able to talk about what she wishes to talk about. This has mainly consisted of elaborating her total incomprehension of what has happened to her emotionally and her childlike approach to managing her life with all the demands upon her that Joey once took care of. The counsellor has learned more about the death and the dreadful wait in the hospital as doctors battled to save his life. Much of the time May has ruminated on the possibility of suing the hotel where Joey slipped on the concrete steps. Even though there was no snow on the steps she is convinced the accident could have been avoided.

Scene Five
Several months later the counselling is still proceeding and May is beginning to talk about seeing a spiritualist. She has met someone who has seen one and was put in touch with her deceased son. May veers between idealising Joey in the sessions and acknowledging how dominant he had been in her life. She seems almost to have been a creation of his – dressing how he wanted her to dress, cooking what he wanted and sharing all the hobbies and sports he enjoyed so

enthusiastically. Joey was her first boyfriend and only real friend. The couple socialised but with his friends and their girlfriends or wives. May wonders when she will be 'rejoining' Joey and talks about it as if it were an appointment which had been booked but the time has been forgotten. Sometimes the counsellor feels as if there is nothing he can do to help her. She also speaks of her family and the way her parents do not know what to say to her when she visits, unlike her counsellor, and she smiles lovingly at him as she says this.

Despite the difficulties involved in helping May to come to terms with her loss and to help her with the crisis in her own development that it has precipitated, the counsellor is quite pleased with his work so far, though he finds May to be rather superficial and feels that he is less successful with her than with most clients. However, he has been asked by the management committee if he will take over the new training programme for voluntary counsellors and a supervision group for established counsellors. He will need to reduce his counselling to make a space for these projects which are very interesting to him. May has hardly begun to move through the stages of grieving when he is faced with a choice of terminating the counselling or turning down an exciting opportunity. He is thinking that perhaps she could be referred to a bereavement group which a volunteer is trying to set up. He would need to present this to her carefully and feels the time for ending altogether is a long way off. He is also aware of his own attraction to May.

Ongoing work
Six months after the beginning of counselling, May is still meeting individually with the counsellor on a weekly basis. He had been very tempted to persuade May to join the new group that had been forming and had raised it as an option. She had been curious and suggested that she could think about it when she felt ready to try something different. She said that she liked helping people though she did not have a great deal of experience. The counsellor realised that May had not understood that he meant her to be a member of the group. He sensed that she was far from ready to transfer to a group and would probably need individual support for a time if she were ever to transfer. Furthermore, it dawned on the

counsellor that they were moving towards the first anni-versary of Joey's death and that this would be a critical moment for May.

He decided to work an extra night at the agency in order to be able to run the training course. He postponed running the supervision group for six months when he reckoned he would be able to move to fortnightly meetings with his two other more long-standing clients. Fortnightly sessions and monthly sessions were often used towards the end of a significant period of counselling. He felt some resentment when he made this decision but soon forgot about it as his work proceeded and his role in the agency became more influential.

May arrived fractionally late for the session which was arranged to take place on the first anniversary of Joey's death. She looked pale and tired. She said very little and the counsellor found tears welling in his eyes. They had talked previously about how to mark this special anniversary. May had decided that she and her family would go with Joey's parents and relatives to plant a tree for Joey in a local park, on the route he often took when he went running. The tree planting became a complicated business with much doubt about the kind of tree, the location and the plaque. May consulted everybody and there were some family arguments. In the end she plumped for a lime, though most people wanted a willow. She knew that Joey loved the smell of lime trees when he ran past them in the summer. She worried that she would say the wrong things at the ceremony and was nervous.

When May told her counsellor about the day ahead and what was planned she took on a faraway look. The coun-sellor shared with her his feeling that she was thinking about something else as she spoke. She smiled and said she thought her husband was in the room with them, in fact he had been there before but she was too embarrassed to admit it. The counsellor felt the hair rising on his neck. May looked at him and said, 'I know he's not really there but he is.' She had told the counsellor before about how she liked to talk to Joey when she came home from work but that she often felt sad because he wasn't there in reality. On the anniversary of his death, the eve of their wedding anniversary, she felt, as she had on some other occasions, that he was strongly present. The counsellor experienced a close bond between them on that

*day and couldn't help shedding a tear. It had been a long
time since the loss of his own brother in a car crash, in
which he too had been involved, had brought him into
bereavement counselling. But on days such as this it felt as if
it were only yesterday.*

Ending
*Two years after commencing counselling May is leaving the
premises of the bereavement agency after her last session. She
has made plans to go to university in her home town. She is
still quite isolated but night school in the last year has given
her a greater sense of confidence. She misses Joey and has not
wanted to meet anyone else, though all her family have
suggested that she should be looking for a new partner. She is
still angry with the hotel where the accident occurred and is
rather disillusioned about spiritualism. She has learned that
many people are horrified when they find out about her loss
and do not want to speak to her. Relations with colleagues at
work have improved a little but she is keen to move on to more
interesting work when she has completed her education. She
is tearful when she says goodbye to her counsellor and gives
him a scented plant as a gift.*

Discussion

The kind of counselling that May is offered in this example is
special in several ways. The counselling is provided by a voluntary
body and counsellors are trained inhouse to work with clients who
are bereaved. The counselling may be of a professional standard
but does not constitute paid employment. This means that the
counsellor's motivation to continue with the work is not supported
by financial incentives, though voluntary agencies that train counsellors often provide an opportunity to develop skills and gain
experience which can be very hard to find elsewhere. The benefits
to a counsellor's career can be substantial, especially in the early
days when people who want to work therapeutically and do not
have a core 'caring' profession need to learn how to help other
people. It may be the case that counselling another person over
time is one of the main ways in which a counsellor learns his or her
trade and this heuristic factor is a big incentive in newly qualified
counsellors. May's counsellor is clearly very experienced and has

to face the choice of ending the counselling relationship prematurely or sacrificing his career development. His solution is a responsible one – he continues to work with his client. There are times when the choice is not as simple and an ideal solution is not possible. Anyone who wishes to work over time with a client pays a price for it which is an aspect of long-term counselling unrecognised by some advocates of short-term counselling. Feltham (1997), for example, constantly refers to the financial rewards for counsellors who work long-term. More about the commitment involved in long-term counselling will be discussed in Chapter 6.

In May's case, the contract which is entered into with the client is open-ended and yet starts from a very specific focus. Bereavement counsellors make use of concepts such as stages of bereavement and transitory states of mind which cannot be hurried out of the way (see Kübler-Ross, 1981; Worden, 1983; Parkes, 1985 for excellent further reading). Bereavement counselling is a good example of how some counselling, with some clients or some kinds of difficulties simply cannot be carried out without the benefit of time. This is not to say that deliberate premature termination of therapeutic help is never possible (see Parsons, 1982) but it is often not appropriate.

The bereaved client's adaptation to the changed reality after a sudden and shocking death such as Joey's needs time to take place. May's dependent personality and the reluctantly articulated tensions between May and Joey, taken together with the untimeliness of the death and Joey's young age, could have added up to a picture of an unresolved grief. (For further reading about the risks of a complicated grief reaction and the danger of suicide in a situation like May's, see Greenblatt, 1978; Worden, 1983: 98–101.) Relatives and colleagues who were unable to bear the painfulness of May's loss were keen to encourage her to get over the death quickly and were at a loss for words with which to comfort her. A counsellor who demonstrated an equivalent pressure for May to adapt would be taking time out of the healing 'equation' of therapeutic relationship, client, counsellor and time united together to bring about the outcome of change or cure or healing. The counsellor has also needed time to establish emotional contact with May and to learn from his own feelings. When something is unthinkable or inexpressible, time alone will not necessarily help its realisation, but without time there can be no process of emotional learning. Such thinking is commonplace among bereavement counsellors who would expect some bereft persons to need several years of grieving, though not necessarily such extended counselling. However, as readers will surely know, once a relationship is established in counselling the focus of concern which brings a client for help will almost certainly shift. How the counsellor chooses to relate to a deepening and widening focus will differ on many counts: orientation, setting, client, contract, training, experience. In Chapter 6 we will return to this subject in relation to May.

The nature of time is an issue in May's case. The counsellor, for example, explicitly became aware of the dissolution of encapsulated time when he remembered his own brother's death. His adaptation to the loss of his sibling did not preclude him from strong feelings of sadness and grief when May spoke about Joey being present with them. Special times such as birthdays, Christmas or anniversaries expose the linear sense of time as a rather inadequate concept when it comes to understanding people's distress. May spent a long period of time attached to a need to blame the hotel for the accident. Another client may have moved through this well-documented stage of anger in bereavement more quickly. May was surrounded by people who wanted to help her progress at a faster speed as if there was a fixed quotient of time allocated to different problems in life. However, the unconscious knows no sense of time and after a bereavement continues to operate as if loved ones who have died are about to return.

Conclusion

Although we have tried to present a range of clients, issues and settings it is obviously impossible to illustrate every conceivable setting, difficulty or way of working in only six examples. We have chosen to describe a few cases in some depth rather than to attempt (and fail) to give a fully comprehensive account. We should however like to draw attention to some significant omissions before ending this chapter in order to give an indication of the many forms that long-term counselling can take and the variety of people it may help.

Long-term counselling is not restricted to the settings we describe in this chapter. We have given no illustrations from schools, social work practice or psychology departments, many of which do provide some long-term work. We have offered no examples of successful counselling in private practice, although this is the setting for much long-term work, especially given current constraints in the public and voluntary sectors.

All of the clients described here are comparatively young but we should certainly not wish to imply that counselling is only for those in the first half of their lives; older people can and do benefit. In presenting more women than men and a predominance of white clients we are, we think (no accurate statistics are available) reflecting something of the reality of those currently offered or asking for counselling, but we do not wish to imply approval of these imbalances.

Some of the clients described in this chapter come for help reluctantly at first (Tom, Julia, Pamela) and all with little clear sense of what counselling can and cannot offer. This does not have to be the case; many clients do come with fairly accurate expectations of counselling gained from either previous helpful experiences or general education. All of our six examples are driven to seek help because of an immediate and pressing difficulty which is clearly hampering their ability to function in their everyday lives. The point at which people seek counselling is always significant, but many clients manage their lives satisfactorily despite being conscious of unfulfilled potential and disharmony within themselves. They may come at a particular developmental stage – for example, mid-life or retirement – with a wish to take stock of and find perspective on past and future. Some may wish to explore their internal worlds, to muse about the significance of their dreams, feelings and fantasies as well as trying to change external situations. Such people often make good use of counselling.

The next chapter will offer a thorough discussion of the issues around assessment for long-term counselling. In this chapter we have indicated some kinds of people who might benefit by being offered time to change or at least to stabilise. They tend to bring long-standing concerns which may have been forced on their attention by a particular life event or difficulty in coping. They are or can become motivated to engage in the process with the counsellor and they are not so vulnerable as to be at risk of being damaged by the necessary frustrations of the work. We have emphasised the need for a fit between the counsellor's competence and the client's needs.

4

How to Assess?

This chapter focuses on assessment where, at least in principle, long-term counselling might be available and where the main task is to make sure that it is appropriate for both client and counsellor. Both parties need to understand and agree that it is what they want.

Assessment is a woefully inadequate word – there ought to be an alternative term to signify the subtle mix of activities and edge-of-awareness processes involved in finding out whether or not the person with whom you are faced should become a client you meet with for a considerable part of your life, to work together in a way that you have yet to establish. Assessments are demanding for the counsellor but can be rewarding as an opportunity to bring all your qualities and abilities to bear on witnessing another person's struggles in life and trying to help them find a way of learning from their experience.

However, being assessed in any way can be very upsetting for the client as it may arouse fears of a potential failure or possible inadequacy of some kind (job interviews and exams are both examples of where an assessment is often associated with anxiety). Clients will often feel nervous about what to expect and fearful of being exposed. The potential for a damaging experience and how to minimize it needs to be uppermost in the counsellor's mind when thinking through how to ensure that the people who are taken in for longer term counselling are the ones who can benefit from it. Where there is no satisfactory help available or referral feasible, both client and professional may find the interaction distressing. First meetings with clients go hand in hand with some preparation for the idea that the relationship might be ongoing or not. In the latter case advice about alternative forms of help should be given, where possible. Some people prefer the term 'exploratory meeting' or 'intake interview', though these are not particularly apt expressions either.

The suggestion that a preliminary meeting may not lead to ongoing work is a subtle business. It is often helpful to stress that the counselling dyad needs to work out what would be best for the client and whether or not the counsellor is the best person to help the enquirer. The phonecalls and first meetings that counsellors have with clients convey a strong impression of how we see our work, ourselves and our clients and contribute to the general public's appraisal of our contribution.

There is already a number of useful books, chapters and journal articles (although overwhelmingly about assessment for psychotherapy) which are excellent (see, for example, Storr, 1979: 6–15; Coltart, 1987: 127–34; Mace, 1995; Malan, 1995: 232–79 and Elton Wilson, 1996: 48–68). The problem in distinguishing who may be suitable for long-term individual counselling, whether humanistic, psychodynamic or integrative, summons up all the prickly issues about parameters, orientation and who does what which were discussed in Chapter 2. Person-centred counsellors are more concerned with empowering clients rather than treating them. Therefore assessment, with its unavoidable association with treatment, is a problematic concept. Yet all counsellors wish to avoid giving the impression that long-term counselling is an anodyne activity, suitable for anyone at any time in their life. Meeting with prospective new clients is a privilege and putting together a picture of the client, his or her capacity to change and the contribution that the counsellor may be able to make, can be a fascinating and complex subject to consider.

Before meeting

In some ways assessment, which is a mutual business even if this is not made explicit, starts even before the client and counsellor meet since clients will have preconceived ideas about the counsellor and how he or she practises. In some instances, clients may have already begun to have formed an opinion about the counsellor, through stories they have heard, clues they detect in the agency's presentation and its location, information gleaned from a phonecall to make an appointment, expectations they bring with them about the value of 'talking'. Some counsellors may be party to procedures whereby they receive written or verbal information about prospective clients, though many prefer to wait until they have actually met before consulting letters of referral or recommendations in order to prevent prejudging of the client. All these background details are an important part of preparing the client and the counsellor for working together and should be considered carefully. Often a telephone call from someone seeking counselling may not result, at the time, in an appointment with the counsellor. However, any initial contact will interact with the caller's fears, hopes and prejudices and set up the beginnings of a transference or expectation which a counsellor will encounter if counselling ever does start and whether he or she wishes to work with it or not. This is true for any sort of counselling, but there are some particular issues involved with long-term helping which need to be identified.

Clients who are thinking of approaching a counsellor may not have in mind the idea that it may take a long time to work towards a satisfactory resolution of their difficulties, nor are they likely to be familiar with the concept of an assessment or preliminary interview. Clients may also be surprised if they have to wait for a first meeting. Long-term work often involves both these requirements. Managing the induction of the prospective client into the counselling 'arena' may occur through direct contact or through literature about the agency or service. It will thus begin a two-way process whereby clients assess whether or not they have approached the right place or person for help and the counsellor is given the chance to begin to form an understanding of the client.

It is right at the beginning that the central features involved in assessment gradually emerge in microcosmic form: a need to take both a subjective and objective view of the client (Holmes, 1995: 28); a need to gain a realistic picture for both the counsellor and the client of what may be possible without losing the hopeful optimism that often accompanies a new client (linking the best in psychodynamic and humanistic tradition respectively, as is suggested by Elton Wilson, 1996: 49); creating an opportunity for each party to sample the other and to get a taste of what working together would be like.

Simple and clear information is required at the outset when the first arrangements are made and the therapeutic alliance begins to be forged. This may be as basic as times available, frequency, cost, and a very rudimentary description of what is involved or a more extended discussion. This can be done in person or on the phone or through explanatory leaflets and booklets such as those produced by the BAC. Some counsellors send out preliminary questionnaires to new clients while others prefer to wait until a face-to-face meeting before proceeding any further. All these procedures hold for any counselling contact. However, when assessment is to take place clients need to be informed in advance and to know that they, too, will be actively involved in the process of evaluating whether they have found the right person or approach for themselves and that ongoing counselling may not automatically ensue. Any limits to how long counselling may continue should also be made clear. Some agencies put an upper limit of two years on counselling contracts.

First meeting

A first interview will be an opportunity for the dual functions mentioned above to come into play as well as a therapeutic experience in itself. Assessments have a double-sided quality in several ways as the following pairs of considerations convey: we have used these as headings to help readers to think through the different issues for themselves. We have structured this chapter around eight different dimensions in relation to which counsellors may wish to position themselves. Hopefully, whatever the counsellor's orientation or attitude to assessment, he or she will be able to conduct the interview without burdening the client with too much closed questioning in relation to these underlying concepts. These dimensions to structure thinking about assessment include:

1 An informal–formal approach.
2 A subjective–objective view of the client.
3 An optimistic–realistic expectation.
4 Practical–emotional issues.
5 A taste of counselling–an evaluation of suitability.
6 Opening up–closing down a therapeutic space.
7 Contracting in–contracting out.
8 The client's view–the counsellor's view.

Such a list looks daunting to any counsellor and indeed it would be a hard task to attend to all these themes in one meeting as well as to accomplish the overwhelming requirement to listen very carefully and respectfully to what the client is more often than not desperate to talk about and to understand.

Whether or not assessment takes place in a formal way, counsellors will often need between one and three sessions to form an opinion about and respond to a range of concerns. Many counselling relationships take place over only a small number of sessions. There is therefore a consonance between the management of time in short-term work and the assessment for long-term counselling. In both cases, the counsellor needs to be able to focus on what is most important for both the client and the counselling process. Here, the essential values of person-centred counselling, formulated by Rogers as the 'core conditions' for creating a climate of change, are of great import for all counsellors, however they work.

The person-centred notion of the essential worth of every person needs to be a fundamental hallmark of any session with a client, be it assessment or not. It should be made explicit that the value of the person is not in question. Even when this is made clear and the client is carefully prepared for the possibility that counselling may not proceed, there may be a sense of rejection rather than an understanding that counselling with this counsellor, in this setting, at this time and in this way is not a profitable solution. The counsellor's remit goes beyond assessment to altering a potential sense of defeat into a real learning experience.

The manner in which counsellors endeavour to make clients feel respected and accepted differs somewhat in every orientation and need not be outlined here but it is important that the client feels there has been a genuine attempt to understand and to empathise. At a practical level, Thorne (1996: 134) suggests non-verbal communications in person-centred counselling can convey more acceptance than statements which may come across as patronising. Holmes (1995: 30) makes a plea for common courtesy in analytic therapy much as Freud (1913) did in his papers on psychoanalytic technique where he also recommended neutrality and tact. The concept of neutrality, nowadays shorn of connotations of frostiness in manner, perhaps best communicates the counsellor's need to maintain a state of mind which is both receptive but neutral in terms of being open to the full picture and not being locked into one aspect of the client's presentation in the initial interview. Counsellors will also, however, wish to demonstrate their own style of being and working with the client. The dimensions listed above may help us to steer a discussion of assessment over useful ground, though counsellors will decide for themselves which are most useful to them.

An informal–formal approach

It may seem as if an assessment which is carried out very formally is 'real' and scientific, whereas all the other subtle means we have of testing out how accurate we are in understanding another person and working out if we can help them are inferior, less reliable methods. On the contrary, Segal (1993) explain the history of assessment related to the short-term, cognitive-behavioural therapy they endorse (perhaps a useful contrast to the longer term work we are espousing here) and how it grew out of informal anecdotes about clinicians' experience:

> Our observations were initially based on 'soft' sources, such as clinical intuition and therapists' impressions of patients who had difficulty with our approach to CBT. These observations led us to a number of preliminary conclusions. First, patients who were not suitable for short-term CBT, perhaps because a longer or more open-ended form of treatment was indicated, had difficulty with issues around termination. Accepting such patients for treatment did not seem to be in their best interest, because termination which occurred while these patients were still in the midst of working on their concerns would disrupt earlier therapeutic gains. Second, certain styles of patient presentation, regardless of diagnosis, were associated with greater ease in working within this treatment model. (Segal, 1993: 107–8)

Time and again writers from all the different perspectives describe assessment procedures and criteria as emanating from the clinical experience and acumen of practitioners, whether Malan (1995: 233) alluding to assessment skills for psychotherapy arising 'from the way he has to think on his feet', or Thorne (1996: 131) summoning up his own experience of 'clients who are unlikely to be much helped by the approach' (person-centred therapy), or the cognitive-behaviourists quoted above. Tantam (1995: 23) casts doubt upon whether or not practitioners of psychotherapy really do know with which clients they can accomplish satisfactory results and calls for more objective systematic study of selection and assessment. However, the authors believe that the following chapters may well confirm the sense which counsellors already have of when to take on a client for longer term work and when to offer some other alternative, even though we anticipate that we cannot speak to the broad audience we hope will read this book without hitting some false notes.

In Chapter 3, there are no examples of formally conducted assessments, other than Joy's, or psychological tests. This reflects much counselling practice which tends to favour informal assessment for suitability by meeting with a client over a period of time and conducting a trial period of counselling. Alternatively, an almost unstructured interview is offered where the counsellor gives the client the opportunity to speak and be understood and where a 'history' emerges. Taking a formal history and structuring the interview by attention to specific preplanned questions is less common. Some counsellors may see clients who have either been assessed or interviewed by a previous person. Pamela, for example (page 27), was referred by her GP. Her counsellor agreed to see her over a period of time when Pamela was very preoccupied with a crisis in her life. Only as Pamela began to be able to think beyond the immediate problems in her life did the counsellor consider whether or not to suggest a more open-ended arrangement, both in terms of time and the issues which the crisis had thrown up for Pamela. This is an excellent example of how a counsellor may shift from one part of the musical score into another and how a trial period can last for one counselling session or, as in this case, several months. Pamela could have satisfactorily ended her counselling when her daughter returned but the counsellor felt that more help could be offered and could be used. More will be said later about the basis for the counsellor's optimism.

Joy (page 35) was interviewed on 'intake' to the agency where she was seen and deemed suitable for psychodynamic counselling. Though we know something about why she was thought to be suitable, the assessment seems not to have clearly identified childhood sexual abuse as a problem. This is often the case where a direct question about abuse is not asked, demonstrating how the client, too, perhaps might need an extended period of time to test out the emotional safety of the setting and the relationship with the counsellor. In Joy's case an intimate medical examination precipitated the work on abuse, though it could be argued that the trusting relationship with the counsellor facilitated Joy caring more about her body which led to a visit to the Well Woman clinic. Whichever way we interpret this, it is apparent that little explicit attention had been paid to Joy's sexual history at assessment. Perhaps direct questioning would have brought forth this issue at an earlier date or it might have reproduced another trauma for Joy and prompted her to withdraw from counselling.

Individual counsellors will feel differently about the extent to which an assessment should delve into such matters and whether or not to trust the client to disclose what needs to be presented. It may be a distinguishing feature of counselling that there is a tendency to work with what clients bring in a way which is comfortable to them, using skills belonging to the first and second clusters described in Chapter 2 before involving third cluster approaches, if at all. Such an idea would be in keeping with a tendency to opt for a longer period of 'slow' assessment while counselling to meet a very immediate need. The shift from one set of skills to another as the client adapts to counselling may be what Jacobs means when he writes: 'Those who work as both psychotherapist and counsellor may also shift their modus operandi as a client moves from one level of enquiry and insight into another' (1994: 81).

Tom's counsellor takes a family history in a way that strikes Tom as being at odds with his own needs to talk about the more immediate problems at work (page 42). Attention to other aspects of Tom's situation seems to have been lacking such as his hopes and goals for what counselling can achieve – suggesting that a rather incomplete assessment had taken place, whether formal or informal. The counsellor's inexperience seems to be as much a problem as the assessment in this case. Where a structured formal format is involved, the client is given the benefit of a more thoroughgoing and less partial approach. This may be helpful to inexperienced counsellors. Questionnaires which are completed in advance of counselling may be of help to those who feel comfortable with this less personal and direct way of beginning an encounter with a client. They also can prompt advance thinking by the client. If a structured psychological test is used it may offer an alternative clinical picture or alert the counsellor to important issues. Less intrusive may be the use of a checklist after the first meeting where the counsellor can review in private the areas that were covered within the session and the ones which remain unknown, helping the counsellor to identify which specific information to elicit or which trial interventions to attempt. Some counsellors may choose to use a combination of approaches to assessment. At the end of this chapter we have included two checklists which readers may wish to adopt (see box on page 101). Supervision is another important and in some respects quite formal strategy for considering suitability of clients or processing assessment experiences.

David's counsellor assesses his suitability for counselling in an informal yet loosely structured way – shifting between the need to listen and support him and her own need to make sure that she can genuinely help someone who is psychologically fragile and under medical treatment (page 48). She liaises with the GP and takes a long time (most of a term) to complete a trial period of counselling before agreeing to continue to meet with David. In this case, setting goals and making a realistic contract were important features of an informal assessment which was gentle but thoughtfully systematic. Julia's counsellor operates in a similar way, though the trial period is much briefer and the goals are less circumscribed.

May is not assessed as such. Her details are taken over the phone and 'suitability' is gauged simply in terms of her being recently bereaved. Some agencies may require more information and may exclude some categories of people, but this is not the case for May. Her first session is where her counselling begins. Though assessment is not being carried out in the normal sense of the word, something informal about establishing rapport and how the counsellor is to relate to this woman is being developed and fine tuned. Again, the act of trying to set up a counselling relationship determines whether or not the counsellor will feel as if he can work with May in an open-ended or long-term way.

In assessing clients for long-term work it is advisable to take time to make an informed decision, whether based on a formal or informal approach. Clients may also need time to make up their minds. Experienced counsellors may choose one or other approach or perhaps combine some formal 'basic questions' with a lot of opportunity for intuitive responses. It may be argued that inexperienced counsellors could benefit from exposure to some structured approaches to assessment, though not necessarily by using them literally in the session itself. Structures are effective where they save unnecessary effort or prevent mistakes from being made, but they should not be used instead of relating and thinking with the client. This intersubjective aspect of assessment is discussed under the next heading.

A subjective–objective view of the client

In making sure that a long-term approach is helpful for a client, counsellors need to be able to gauge how they feel about the person with whom they are considering undertaking work. They also need to be able to set this against more objective factors which relate to the client. For example, David is a charming young man and his counsellor feels positive about him and that she can probably help him. However, she needs to find out how he has responded to other forms of help in the past, what kind of situations might make him vulnerable and how his medication and relationship to other medical helpers will affect his counselling. Some of this information falls into the category of 'objective view' in that there are known discernible patterns in people's behaviour when they are suffering from certain diagnosable disorders. Counsellors who wish to help clients such as David would do well to make sure that they understand how 'illness' - for want of a better term - intersects with a client's personality. More will be discussed later in relation to the similar issue of balancing optimism against realistic evaluation. However, David's counsellor provides herself with some of this information simply by speaking to David and his GP.

It is entirely possible to use rating systems and psychological tests to formulate a less subjective view of the client's personality or state of mind. This is sometimes carried out where research is being conducted, but generally a more personal encounter is preferred whereby counsellors use their own clinical acumen and sensitivity. At a deep level, the counsellors will be identifying a range of reactions in themselves in relation to the client. This delicate use of the counsellor's self or countertransference is a source of knowledge we tend to prize, though it can be difficult to have a feeling and think about it at the same time. A very strong countertransference feeling (for example, a powerful urge to look after a client) can indicate an identification with an aspect of the client's personality which has been disowned by the client and projected into the counsellor. This is not the same as being able to empathise with a painful emotion but more akin to feeling something for somebody else who wishes to avoid it.

One counsellor remembers a very disturbed and mainly inaudible client who left the first session in a grim state of despair, having agreed to return later in the week. The counsellor felt that she had made contact with an isolated and terrified part of the patient's personality and was probably the first person he had ever really been understood by. She felt she must make sure the client could be seen by her in an open-ended way, though she had not proposed this to the young man. He returned as planned and was able to begin to talk more loudly and to put some of his thoughts and feelings into words. This young man did not have a psychiatric history and apart from presenting himself so quietly showed no overt signs of disorder, though the counsellor could not make sense of his chaotic family background about which he seemed evasive. By the third session, the client was beginning to express himself more confidently and was no longer feeling so hopeless. Instead, he told the counsellor he was beginning to feel rather embarrassed because he had feelings towards her about which he couldn't talk. Over a short period of time these feelings grew into an eroticised transference. The counsellor felt subjectively that this desperate young man would not be suitable for counselling. She began to realise that the powerful urge to rescue him that she had experienced unhelpfully complemented his unconscious desire to ensconce himself in another person who could not only supply him with everything he would ever need but would always be under his control. This young man would have fulfilled the criteria for borderline personality (see page 90).

Such a marked reaction in the counsellor is quite distinct from the other kinds of feelings we monitor in ourselves about clients. May's counsellor was able to acknowledge that he found his client attractive in a girlish sort of way when he first caught sight of her in the waiting room. His feelings were not cause for alarm and signalled an aspect of May's difficulties which could not be discussed for a long time. They presaged a later problem for the counsellor who came to find May very attractive. If you are going to see clients over a long time you need to feel that you can cope with the reality of working with them. The literature on assessment does acknowledge the wealth of feelings a counsellor or psychotherapist may bring to bear in a subjective way on deciding whether or not a counselling contract should be made. However, the literature tends not to make recommendations like: do not take on clients you find overwhelmingly attractive or who you cannot stand, though the authors feel that this is generally good advice. However, you might want to refer such a client to an appropriate colleague who you feel can help. If you are doubtful, it is wise to seek help from supervision. It may also be necessary to revise your initial assessment in the light of working with the client.

Yariv (1995) has described the first impressions made on her by clients and how she used this subjective knowledge correctly to make formulations about the key issues brought by the client. It can be useful to review the first impression created by a client when the counselling is coming to a close and to reconsider what this might have communicated. There is evidence that a good match between the values and beliefs of the counsellor and the client may facilitate a positive outcome (Kelly and Strupp, 1992). It may be advisable for the counsellor who is not experienced in seeing long-term clients to avoid those who seem to be too much out of the 'ordinary' in his or her own practice. Having said this, a long-term client rightly comes to occupy a special place in the counsellor's mind regardless of the first impression.

A good way to think about processing the experience of meeting with a new client for assessment is in terms of left-brain–right-brain thinking. As Mollon (1997) points out, counselling and psychotherapy are essentially emotional experiences which need to be thought about rationally, supervision being one place where the raw emotional experience can be subjected to thought. Tom's counsellor really needed to be able to consider why he was choosing to see him in his private practice; his practical reasons as a trainee counsellor were obvious but not necessarily related to the needs of the client.

Optimistic–realistic expectations

Elton Wilson puts the issues fairly and squarely in regards to this dimension:

> To integrate the optimism of the humanist into the realistic caution of the psychoanalyst and the outcome-oriented scrutiny of the cognitive-behaviourist is an ambitious task. Whether working in brief or long-term psychological therapy, assessment and review are core practitioner skills always in need of refinement. (Elton Wilson, 1996: 49)

This requires an integration of the capacity to relate to each individual as a unique person with the ability to recognise some of the significant facts about them within diagnostic categories. It is also determined by setting. A counsellor in private practice who has no experience of working with someone with a major mental illness and no connection with that client's GP could be setting themselves and their client up for a disappointing, if not disastrous experience (although much always depends on the counselling dyad and their combined capacity to find creative links with each other). An advantage in making some distinctions between parts of the counselling–psychotherapy field, as outlined in Chapter 2, is that it paves the way for some kinds of counselling to be undertaken with people with mental health problems who are normally excluded by suitability criteria for some forms of psychotherapy. Counsellors who work in medical settings, or who have the experience and can offer some help and support to people who they feel sure can use it, should not be deterred by selection criteria which may be valid for some settings but not others, for some 'levels' of counselling and not others, for some goals in outcome and not others.

Rogers worked with schizophrenics at one point in his career, though he later came to the conclusion that person-centred therapy (we do not believe he distinguished it from person-centred counselling) was probably more helpful for people who were reasonably well adjusted to life (Thorne, 1996). Thorne focuses on the limitations of particular counsellors to facilitate the core conditions rather than the client, though he acknowledges some problem clients:

> Such people are usually somewhat rigid and authoritarian in their attitude to life. They look for certainties, for secure structures and often for experts to direct them in how they should be and what they should do . . . Overly intellectual or logically rational people may also find it difficult to engage in the kind of relationship encouraged by person-centred therapy, where often the greatest changes result from a preparedness to face painful and confusing feelings which cannot initially be clearly articulated. Clients falling into these categories often turn out to be poorly motivated in any case. (Thorne, 1996: 131)

Thorne (1996: 131) proposes some positive criteria in selecting clients which emanate from strong motivation for change and asks:

■ Is the client really desirous of change?
■ Is the client prepared to share responsibility for our work together?
■ Is the client willing to get in touch with his or her own feelings, however difficult that may be?

These client qualities are not related specifically to long-term counselling and are consistent with factors which make a client likely to progress with or without help according to Tantam (1995: 18).

Linked to motivation is the capacity to be able to think psychologically about the causes of problems and the remedies for them. Psychological-mindedness is not the same as the capacity to talk as if one understands about emotional and psychological matters when they emerge in counselling. Articulate clients may not be capable of imaginative and emotional reflection or of making links to their own past or to internal emotional states. A trainee psychologist approached a counsellor with a view to embarking on personal counselling to help him understand himself and to give him a taste of what it would be like to be a client. He was able to analyse his psychological state and diagnose himself as having an obsessive personality. He was willing to talk about himself but kept waiting for the counsellor to suggest ways in which he might help himself. Every time the counsellor tried to identify a feeling or to reflect back to him the frustration that seemed to be growing between them he was met by uncomprehending looks and denial. This client had motivation and could express himself in psychological language but could not connect feelings to thoughts or vice versa. Often, it is the counsellor who has to learn the language of the client's emotional life in the most concrete way in a first session. Clients who communicate less confidently may sometimes produce the most stunning insights and personal growth, especially if the counsellor can learn the language of the client's emotional life. Joy seemed to have difficulty in expressing herself at first but soon developed a capacity to use the counselling relationship to reflect upon herself. Joy needed what Winnicott (1958: 53) called 'a period of hesitation' before she could make use of counselling.

Coltart elucidates psychological-mindedness very helpfully and also wonders if the client (or patient in her case as she is talking about assessment for psychoanalytic psychotherapy) has had any success or achievement in any area of life, however limited, and can feel pleased about it. She writes: 'It is an important truism that he who fails at everything will fail at analysis' (1987: 132). Counsellors are rightly more optimistic than psychoanalysts and their aims are less ambitious, but nevertheless there is truth in this statement for clients who may enter counselling. For some people it may be best that they receive only short-term help or a non-psychological form of help such as medication.

The counsellor will be sensing whether or not clients can go on and talk as a result of being listened to or whether they always have to be prompted or attended to very closely to help express themselves. Those clients who need a lot of help to explore may find the non-directive nature of psychodynamic and person-centred counselling frustrating. Sometimes it is a question of a client learning how to perform a client role but it may be that a non-structured, open-ended process of reflection is just not compatible with the client's personality or way of being in the world. How the client responds to the counsellor's attempts at empathy or at making links between experiences and feelings and whether fresh material is prompted by such interventions will be very indicative of how the counselling is likely to fare.

Commonly, within the psychodynamic tradition, diagnostic criteria have been outlined to help deselect inappropriate clients. Malan (1995) has written extensively about assessment of clients for psychodynamic psychotherapy and lists six ways in which the interviewer needs to think and behave. Obviously we have to adapt this list for the purposes of thinking about long-term counselling but it is worthwhile to include here, in summarised form, as Malan's ideas have infused many assessment guidelines (see box below).

Attention to such matters can be couched in other language and with other theoretical frameworks in mind, for example, the person-centred counsellor may view conflict in the relationship between the client's self and the client's self-concept. For the psychodynamic practitioner, the nub of the matter is to weigh up the strengths and weaknesses of the client against the extent to which the client may be overly disturbed by the therapeutic encounter. A client who has attempted suicide must always be very carefully assessed and the kind of counselling offered to such a person must always take into account that an attempt has been made. Malan concludes in language that is not so different from Thorne's:

> With this balance in mind, the interviewer tries to forecast whether the patient will be able to interact with a therapist and face his hidden feelings without serious threats to himself (e.g. suicide), to others (e.g. violence), or to his therapy (severe dependence, uncontrollable acting out). (Malan, 1995: 234)

Malan's summarised guidelines

1 Think about the possibility of psychiatric problems.
2 Think about the meaning of conflicts within the client and between the interviewer and the client and their links with past conflicts in the client's life.
3 Think about how such themes as emerge will affect the future of the therapy if it is to start.
4 Think practically about what is possible in terms of your resources.
5 Create rapport to help you gain access to what you need to know.
6 Take care of the client in the interview and think about what he or she will feel when it is over.

It is this kind of thinking harnessed to the person-centred trust in the capacity for each individual to accomplish their full potential, given the right conditions, which brings about therapeutic optimism allied with realism, though psychodynamic counsellors may feel concern about the more negative feelings which can become unleashed in the counselling process and may harbour more caution.

Who to include and who to exclude
Given the above observations the offer of long-term counselling comes down to some straightforward issues:

- if the client can present problems which the counsellor feels able to work on using the counselling techniques with which he or she is competent;
- if counselling does not constitute a threat to the client as identified by Malan in the quotation above;
- if the counsellor feels he or she can establish rapport and a therapeutic alliance with the client and that the client can make use of the counsellor's approach to helping, as tested out in a trial session or sessions;
- if the client and counsellor are motivated and have the time;
- if there are no obvious reasons why they should not work together.

If these criteria are fulfilled then counselling may well be a long-term proposition.

The range of people who become at risk as clients includes those who are currently mentally ill with conditions such as severe depression and/or psychosis; people with a paranoid personality; people whose symptoms seem to be definitely of a physical kind which cannot be accounted for in purely emotional or psychological ways; alcohol and drug abusers (better left to specialist counsellors); hypochondriacal people and anyone whose behaviour seems to have suddenly changed and become bizarre for no detectable reason.

People with personality problems are often thought to be very difficult to work with and may even fare less well than others in purely medical treatments (Shea et al., 1990, mentioned in Tantam, 1995: 13). Clinical descriptions of the borderline personality and other psychiatric classifications can be found in the ICD-10 (WHO: 1992) and the DSM-IV (APA: 1994). Fonagy's description will, perhaps convey to counsellors the need to be realistic about how much can be achieved with such clients in counselling:

> The relationships they describe appear to be short-lived, sound chaotic yet extremely intense. They manifest an interpersonal hypersensitivity which leads to dramatic alterations in their relationships, a fragmentation of their sense of identity, an overwhelming affective response and mental disorganisation. The features are particularly evident in the transference. Their submissiveness can suddenly turn to disparagement and rage of remarkable intensity. The trigger may be the mildest criticism or the slightest rebuff in the face of what appear to be unreasonable demands for understanding or gratification. (Fonagy, 1991: 639)

Furthermore, people who have experienced mental health problems in the past may also risk becoming very disturbed again in counselling, even when it is gentle and careful. When psychodynamic practitioners talk of a client's ego-strength it simply means the degree to which the ego or the self can hold together under strain and permit the client still to function without deteriorating or breaking down. David is a good example of a manic-depressive person who does benefit from counselling, but where the goals are restricted and where the work avoids undermining his fragile defences against strong feelings and impulses.

Julia has anorexia nervosa. People with eating disorders can be a difficult group of clients to engage in change-oriented work and may need help from a GP as well as a counsellor. Recognising the counsellor's limits is essential. Daines et al. (1997) introduce counsellors to the issues to consider where psychiatric or medical problems are concerned. Pamela has a less disturbing presentation though she does not appear at first to be very psychologically minded and has a history of childhood disruption and many years in care. It takes a good while for Pamela's counsellor to become convinced of the appropriateness of longer term work because she is afraid Pamela will not be able to cope with separation and loss and could break down during holiday breaks when the counsellor's absence might arouse childhood feelings of being punished and sent away. May's counsellor finds her both attractive and oddly childlike. He can understand her state of mind in the context of her bereavement. She does not seem to be particularly psychologically minded, yet seems to benefit from talking to him and has managed to continue coping with her life albeit in a rather dazed fashion so the counsellor feels that counselling is 'right' in this case.

An important category of people for whom there may be severe problems in longer term counselling is those who have never had a positive relationship to another human being over at least some period of time. Alas, such people are desperate for relationships but are unlikely to be able to make use of the therapeutic relationship in order to effect change in their lives and may become as dependent on the counsellor as a patient to a life-support system. This could become lifelong attachment rather than long-term counselling which was one reason why Pamela's counsellor exercised such caution. There is little help available for emotionally deprived people who have never experienced a satisfactory attachment in life and unfortunately there are few agencies which will take responsibilities for managing their needs. GPs often bear the burden of supporting such people although they have little time available in which to do it.

Another reason for referring on a client may be that there are too many chances of the client's personal or professional world and the counsellor's overlapping in a way that would be difficult for either party to manage. A client who works in the same institution or who mixes in the same social circles may later regret having a counsellor for a colleague and the counsellor will almost certainly be inhibited by the special relationship. Psychodynamic counsellors would probably differ from person-centred counsellors in how they see boundaries. The latter might think of boundaries as being within the counsellor's person, asking themselves: 'Am I going to be able to maintain appropriate boundaries with this person?' There are huge differences in how individual counsellors from the person-centred perspective would feel about such matters. Rogers (1967) was, however, clear that the counsellor needed separateness in order to function therapeutically. It is the counsellor's responsibility to make a realistic decision about what can be tolerated as reasonable and unavoidable and what is to be avoided at all costs.

Another note of realism needs to be struck in relation to clients who have seen a lot of helpers in the past without benefit. You may be the best counsellor the client has a chance of meeting and very skilled but it is likely that you will fail as others have. Where clients have had intermittent experiences of counselling from which they feel they have learned something which has changed them, there is more cause for optimism. Although the counsellor and client both need to consider what more counselling can achieve, there may still be useful work to do together.

Practical–emotional issues

How on earth do counsellors manage to hear what the client has to say, give any information they need to give, find out relevant information and test out whether or not their approach is usable by the client, all within a limited amount of time? (See checklists, page 101.)

Again, some information can be sought in advance but most counsellors prefer simply to take basic details such as: name; address; contact telephone number; GP's name, address and phone number (where appropriate); how they came to be referred and by whom (also where appropriate). Depending on the setting, other questions are asked of clients such as date of birth, marital status, occupation, dependants and so on. Counsellors need to give clients an explicitly agreed amount of time for the session so that they know how long they have and to encourage them to explain what they are seeking help for and why at this point in their life. Where a long-term contract is not the only choice, the counsellor may not take very much information from the client though it is important to do so at a later point if the counselling is to continue.

A formally structured history taking is rare though may be helpful in some circumstances, such as with a client who presents in a chaotic way. Key questions interposed in the session will elicit most relevant information that does not just tumble out of the interview on its own. Asking clients to tell you something about their family background or their current home situation or what they think are the reasons they have the difficulties they are faced with usually produces abundant material. It may be necessary to ask if clients have sought help before and how they got on with it, what the worst moments have been like for them and, if there is a previous history, what was helpful then. Similarly, direct questions may be asked about medication where this seems appropriate and the beginnings of an exploration into situations when the client may need to give permission for liaison with the GP. Depending on the orientation of the counsellor, information over a range of other issues may either be sought or simply gathered as it emerges. Sources of support, relationships including intimate ones, losses, dreams, plans for the future – counsellors should be able to find out enough about their new client to help them make the kind of assessment that fits with their own method and helps them forecast whether long-term work is a valid option.

Much of the time, though, the client is keen to focus on the immediate issue for which help is being sought. The counsellor is faced with both attending to the emotional needs of the client, making sure the client feels they have encountered a thoughtful person who can respond to them in the immediate 'here and now' as well as needing to take note of important information. Writing down notes, other than very basic details of address and so on, is not a good idea in our view and distracts the counsellor as much as the client. Person-centred counsellors will certainly not wish to respond to their clients from outside the client's frame of reference, nor do other counsellors wish to disrupt the client's own narrative process unduly. Logistically, managing the session is a skilled process. Holmes (1995: 29) compares it to a friendly game of chess with opening moves, a middle section of trial interventions and the endgame of gathering together the threads of the conversation and formulating a decision about what happens next.

The counsellor will also need to leave enough time at the end of the first session for a summary or other interventions or to make arrangements with the client. The client will also need to ask questions, some of them very practical. The answers to such questions need careful thought – much is communicated in them and your answers will be very significant. None of the comments made so far pertain solely to long-term work. Other aspects such as making clear arrangements for breaks, holidays, contracting length of time, method and amount of payment where it is made and payment for cancellations are more specifically at issue in long-term work. The need to complete all the practical tasks can feel in conflict with the emotional climate which the counsellor needs to establish for the counselling. An assessment session may demand a great deal of skilled management from a counsellor and can seem arduous. It may also be the first time the client ever feels truly listened to and taken seriously and can be both frightening and intensely painful. On the other hand, it may also restore morale and hope in the client and be experienced as a huge relief and a new beginning.

A taste of counselling–an evaluation of suitability

There is a tension between the need to give the client a taste of counselling and attention to preparation and appropriate selection. This inherent tension can be resolved in several ways. The assessment can be planned to take place over several sessions which are each comparable to a normal experience of the counselling. Such sessions introduce the client to the length of time to be spent together and enable the counsellor to model the approach and style. The counsellor can make a few trial interpretations or use other skills or qualities appropriate to the work in hand and the theoretical orientation. Alternatively, a long (say two-hour) assessment can be made (this has the disadvantage of not including a break between sessions and is a different experience to the usual approach). Or shorter term counselling can begin, as it did for Pamela, for example, and can be brought to a natural ending point before long-term counselling is suggested. There are strong reasons for the assessor to be the person who sees the client when long-term help is being considered, though this is often not possible in large agencies or where trainees are placed. Trainees and clients do benefit from a more experienced counsellor carrying out the assessment and ensuring that there is not too much discrepancy between what a client wants and a trainee can deliver and skilled assessment can allow for the most experienced counsellor taking on the most difficult work. However, the deeper level of personality matching and mutual attunement is necessarily lost when the counsellor is not the assessor and there is the additional responsibility of helping the client make the transition to the new relationship.

It may be the case that counselling literature, questionnaires and self-reports which have been given to clients can cut down on the time needed to exchange information but sometimes such methods of communication can feel dead to the counsellor. They are not in his or her mind in the same way as the words of the client.

It may be necessary to make some interventions which cut across the grain of a session. An example would be where the counsellor might want to test out whether or not the client can bear to be confronted in any way. This may seem heartless but can prevent clients being overly supported in a way that would not prepare them for the tough time that at some point or other may emerge for them in their counselling.

Perhaps the most difficult aspect of the experience for the counsellor to manage is to make sure that a representative sample of counselling is experienced by clients but that where it seems likely a continuation of counselling will not occur, the clients should not feel as if they have started up a process designed to leave them feeling more vulnerable and even more desperate after it is over. Interpretations or empathic responses should be calibrated at a level which respects the temporariness of the therapeutic relationship. Pamela's counsellor (see page 30), for example, is careful not to dive into the painful depths of her abandonment in childhood, which can only be approached very tentatively over time when she is able to bear the pain of thinking about it.

Opening up the therapeutic space–closing it down

The client's suitability may become clear at first meeting and the assessment rapidly becomes a first session like many others. An example would be where a client has been appropriately referred after short-term help. Where counselling is definitely not to ensue, the counsellor faces a difficult task. It is tempting to prevaricate over turning down a client as it can be hurtful and potentially shame-making for both parties. The counsellor needs time to think through what he or she is going to say within the session. The more careful has been the management of preliminary

enquiries before the session was booked, the more likely it is that
the reasons for not offering long-term counselling will be personal
and difficult to convey, especially where it has been specifically
requested. This can be just as true for making a decision when
counselling has been underway for some time. There is nothing
like the plain truth in these difficult situations, though declining to
take on a client for long-term work must always be carried out
with sensitivity and tact. It can be useful to rehearse mentally
some of the expressions that can be used. It is a good idea to
prepare the client before the first session with the idea that
counselling is useful for some but not everyone and that both
client and counsellor need to be able to get a sense of whether or
not they can work together. Clients should not be protected from
the knowledge that it is possible with any form of help to get
worse or to waste a lot of time and effort (not to mention money
where a fee is involved) in pursuing goals which cannot be
acheived.

A client who had stabbed a previous lover was very keen to
explore his behaviour and his motives with a counsellor, especially
as he found himself so bereft without his partner who refused to
see him again. He had been punished for his crime and had
eventually started a new life but could not cope with work and felt
depressed. He was offered a short counselling contract of six
sessions which was the norm in the workplace setting where the
counsellor worked. The client worked very hard and honestly to
face what he had done and impressed the counsellor with his
sincerity and commitment. The client wanted and could have been
given further sessions but the counsellor felt that there could be a
risk of violence in the future when the transference might become
less positive. The client was upset and reassured the counsellor
that he would be able to control his feelings if they became hostile.
The counsellor had to admit to the client that she was not so
certain and that she preferred not to put either of them, or the good
work they had done together, at risk. Not all clients would have
been able to hear this opinion without becoming angry and
possibly aggressive.

On the other hand, counsellors also need to use their diplomacy
and tact in offering long-term work as clients may feel they must be
very disturbed if the counsellor thinks they need so much time.
Tom may have felt that he had been singled out as needy and
unstable when offered longer term counselling.

Some approaches may benefit your client more than your own and you will need to familiarise yourself with potential resources for onward referral. In the discussion about Joy's counselling, some alternatives to long-term counselling such as groupwork or cognitive analytic therapy were considered. Joy's counsellor, in fact, opted to offer Joy more sessions, perhaps recognising that even where relevant, a referral elsewhere can seem like being rejected or passed on like a parcel. Where sexual abuse has occurred the client is likely to feel as if there is something unacceptable about themselves and that a referral to someone else is proof that they are beyond redemption. In private practice, it is essential to know about other practitioners who work in a different way as well as colleagues who you feel might have the special skills for some kinds of clients. In private practice especially, you may need to be able to discuss a problematic situation with a psychiatrist or a general practitioner. Making a referral to someone who is a psychiatrist needs a lot of thought – it can be terrifying and insulting to a client who feels, rightly or wrongly, that this is not appropriate. A friendly relationship with members of a psychiatric or community mental health team in your area is a good idea whichever setting you work in.

Contracting in–contracting out

The contract is the outcome of the assessment. As well as involving the practical arrangements which have already been mentioned, it should involve some consideration of goals. This need not be made explicit in a detailed way but both counsellor and client need to have an idea about how the work is to take place and what the point of it is. This is much easier to assert than to elucidate. Rogers writes about the ideal of the fully functioning person. Thorne (1996: 130) quotes Frick who lists the shifts towards this ideal state and points out that any one of them could constitute a valid endpoint for counselling:

1 away from facades and the constant preoccupation with keeping up appearances
2 away from 'oughts' and an internalised sense of duty springing from externally imposed obligations
3 away from living up to the expectations of others
4 towards valuing honesty and 'realness' in oneself and others
5 towards valuing the capacity to direct one's own life

6   towards accepting and valuing one's self and one's feelings
     whether they are positive or negative
7   towards valuing the experience of the moment and the process of
     growth rather than continually striving for objectives
8   towards a greater respect for and understanding of others
9   towards a cherishing of close relationships and a longing for more
     intimacy
10   towards a valuing of all forms of experience and a willingness to
     risk being open to all inner and outer experiences however
     uncongenial or unexpected. (Frick, 1971: 179)

Psychodynamic practitioners may agree with the extensive list
above but also aim for some more immediate goals, for example, a
reduction in symptoms. Often the problem which brings a person
to counselling ceases to be the main issue after a short time and
making sense of oneself and one's conflicts, in relation to what has
initiated the counselling, becomes a more meaningful goal. It is
well known that Freud thought that transforming hysterical misery
into common unhappiness was an aim of psychoanalysis with one
famous patient but fewer people realise he added: 'With a mental
life that has been restored to health you will be better armed
against that un-happiness' (Freud and Breuer, 1895: 393). Freud
later thought the goals of psychoanalysis should, among others, be
to be able to love and work. Psychodynamic counsellors may be
pleased to settle for shifts towards their ultimate goals, to what
Glueck (1960) called proximate goals which are more immediately
achievable.

The agreement not to go further does not always end at that
point. A client may wish to return at a later date when external
circumstance (such as pregnancy or house move, for example)
have altered. The counsellor needs to think carefully about how a
vague promise to see someone later can, in practice, be kept and
must prepare the client for the wait that will almost certainly ensue.
If the counselling does not proceed for other reasons, clients may
ask for a written assessment to take with them to another agency or
to seek help elsewhere. The counsellor needs to consider whether
or not she is willing to do this and how to negotiate an appropriate
response to the request. The limits of confidentiality need to be
negotiated too – other counsellors may wish to enquire about a
client who has been referred. Clients should be able to feel they
understand and agree to any breaks in confidentiality both during
and after the counselling relationship has ended.

The client's view–the counsellor's view

So far we have tended to place more emphasis on the counsellor's view of the client than the client's view of the counsellor. Yet research shows that the first three sessions are critical in terms of how the counsellor is perceived and whether or not the client feels any hostility from the counsellor, the experience of which is associated with low success rate (Henry and Strupp, 1994). This means that the foundations for the therapeutic alliance are being laid down right from the first moment that the counselling dyad has any contact of any kind with each other – a good relationship is unlikely be be constructed after the assessment if it has not been established in a rudimentary way right from the start. Long-term counselling does give more time in which to pick up and repair difficulties in the alliance which have been detectable at assessment, provided the client stays the course. 'Palatability' (Tantam, 1995: 21) of the 'treatment' and of the counsellor's personal approach and style greatly affect drop-out rate and can be difficult to tease apart. Henry and Strupp discovered in their extensive research on the therapeutic alliance as studied from a basically psychodynamic perspective:

> For the low-outcome [low success] patients, regardless of initial prognosis, therapist behaviour was characterised by a high level of 'negative attitude' and low warmth, which got worse across the first three sessions. Finally, of particular interest were the patients with low prognosis and high outcome. In these cases, positive outcome seemed to be a function of increasing participation by the patient that paralleled increases in therapist warmth and exploration. (Henry and Strupp, 1994: 59)

Sadly Henry and Strupp go on to suggest that additional training designed to improve alliance-making skills has been found to be unsuccessful. Clearly, whatever the orientation of the counsellor, their interpersonal skills and ability to establish rapport are decisive for many clients at assessment, just as research bears out that non-specific factors linked to the counsellor's personal qualities are important to effectiveness. There are good counsellors and psychotherapists and then there are the rest. However, trainees need clients to work with and novice counsellors need to gain experience before they can become good counsellors. The needs of Tom's counsellor who was in training seem to have over-whelmed his appraisal of what was needed and to have become entangled with Tom's problems with authority. The end result is a repetition of an unsatisfying relationship with someone who is supposed to be a reliable and caring figure for Tom. Furthermore, the counsellor starts off his private practice with an experience of failure.

Clients will need time to ask questions as outlined in the section above about practical versus emotional issues. However, some of the questions posed, if not all, will be full of significance which goes beyond their manifest content. One client who presented for help asked about the counsellor's success rate. In some ways this was a very pertinent question. The counsellor explored with the client the possible fears and expectations which were wrapped up in this question as well as giving some idea of the benefits and limitations of the help that was on offer, stressing that success could not automatically be guaranteed (while noting internally how discomfiting was the question and how inappropriate it would feel to declare a high success rate). Tentative explorations and interpretations around the transference, especially the fear that the counsellor might not be good enough or might be too good, were unproductive. The counselling pair met over a trial period which was productive in that it helped the client over a difficult period and demonstrated to both parties that a longer term approach, which in this case would have been psychodynamic, would probably be inadvisable. The client's experience of a trial period of counselling was useful and helped her feel supported and understood but what she wanted long-term was a more goal-directed approach and she was referred for cognitive-behavioural therapy.

Conclusion

The aim of any assessment is above all to do no harm, to avoid offering counselling inappropriately and to make sure clients are able to use the particular approach. The long-term commitment involved should be mediated by an ongoing capacity to review the work and to make this aspect explicit and shared, whether in terms of micro trials of the approach or a lengthier assay or throughout the whole course of the counselling relationship. The client needs to be able to assess the counsellor and the two need to be able to establish a realistic but hopeful sense of purposeful meeting and exploration. It may indeed, be a characteristic of counselling that the counsellor will work with what the client brings rather than work to a pre-ordained plan about what constitutes the remit of counselling or the approach to be used. Different counsellors and different orientations will, nevertheless, place realistic limits on what is possible or desirable in each unique case. Supervision will be a vital part of this process.

Checklist of content and contract

- Have you got all the personal information you need about a client such as full name, address, phone number, GP's details?
- Do you know about the client's present circumstances such as occupation, current family, support system?
- Do you understand what the client's central concerns seem to be about?
- Is there a history to these concerns? If so, when and how did they become important? Has there been previous help and did it work?
- Have you got a picture of the family of origin of your client?
- Have you thought about whether your client might fit the description of clients who should be excluded?
- Can you formulate the problem(s) on which you need to work with your client and can you set goals? Can you picture a satisfactory ending?
- Will you need to liaise with other professionals and if so has the client given you permission to do so?
- Have you got sufficient reason to believe that the client can make good use of your counselling approach?
- Have you grounds for making a clear contract?
- Can you manage this work and would you like to?
- Do you have adequate supervision?

Checklist of process

- How did the client respond to your comments or interpretations?
- Did rapport deepen as the interview proceeded?
- Were there any silences? What did they feel like?
- At what point in the interview did the client appear more upset/ defended/animated?
- Body language? Audibility? Eye contact? What do they mean?
- What kind of response did you get to the suggestion that the work might be long-term?
- How did you feel during the interview? What might this tell you about the client?

5

Day-to-day Considerations

And what you thought you came for
Is only a shell, a husk of meaning
From which the purpose breaks only when it is fulfilled
If at all.

(T.S. Eliot, *Four Quartets*, 1959: 50)

It is not easy to predict how long-term work with someone is going to turn out – the very essence of the work is that time is given so that what is not immediately knowable can emerge. If the counsellor has assessed the client thoughtfully and formed an insight into what might follow in counselling, he or she will still not be sure of the specific quality of the relationship which is to develop. Any relationship that brings no surprises with it would be rather dull and lifeless. However, when a counsellor decides to opt for an open-ended or long-term contract with a client some likely patterns to the work can be discerned. The counsellor can plan for these so that unfavourable surprises will be minimised. This chapter will divide the work into three broad categories: a beginning, a middle and an end. In Chapter 4 an analogy was made to a game of chess by Holmes (1995: 29) when he described the opening and closing moves in relation to the micro-counselling of an assessment session. We prefer to use the analogy of a journey to describe long-term counselling, where, if everything goes well, everyone is altered in the process and no one loses.

Starting out

Obtaining referrals

While we do not recommend advertising in the crude sense, we do think it may be worthwhile to let potential referrers know that a service may be available for clients whose psychological needs or personal growth can best be met through longer term counselling. Despite the lengths to which we went in Chapter 2 to explain that counselling can involve long-term work and be much more than an approach that focuses on immediate concerns, many referrers will be unaware of the full potential (or the limitations) of counselling. Counsellors may wish either to write to or telephone local agencies or produce literature for potential clients which explains briefly and realistically the kind of resource that is available, its cost and how it is accessed. It is advantageous to mention accreditation where it exists both to demonstrate the professional level of counselling practice and to show the counsellor belongs to professional bodies which represent ethical practice. Such bodies are seen by the public to protect the interests of both clients and referrers. Registration is rapidly gaining ground among counsellors and referrers often feel more confident in making referrals to someone unfamiliar where accrediting organisations have deemed the counsellor to be acceptable.

Receiving referrals

When a referral is made it should be considered carefully. In the early days of private practice or when setting up a new service, counsellors can be tempted to take on unsuitable cases or to see people at inconvenient times. Difficulties at the beginning of the counselling relationship to which the counsellor does not pay attention will most surely amplify and augment as time goes on. The establishment of a counselling contract and setting up of a secure frame for the work begins well before the client gets into the consulting room. The way referrals are taken and whether or not the counsellor has a policy of replying to referral letters, the level of formality in making referrals and accepting them all go towards creating the climate in which the work will flourish or founder.

Assessment has been discussed in the previous chapter and will not be revisited here except to remind readers that referrers may also wish to know what has happened after the assessment. Where such knowledge does not serve the interests of the client or the client does not wish the referrer to be involved further, the counsellor needs to tread carefully. Some counsellors would think it important to let the client's GP know (with the client's permission) that their patient has started counselling; others may not see this as appropriate. As a rule of thumb, we would suggest that a counsellor who sees a client with serious mental health problems or who is taking psychotropic medication should recognise that others may be very important in the care of the client and may need to be contacted at some point. There may be times when this is advisable when the client is not in agreement. Such crisis times will be discussed later but it is important to think about them before a critical situation arises. They are much easier to manage if there is already a contract agreed in the event of an emergency situation.

On occasion clients may be very anxious about any contact with a GP because of fears that there will be something in the medical records which will cause them to suffer unwanted repercussions. Numerous examples come to mind: the client who is HIV positive and fears breakdown of confidentiality and victimisation; the medical student who fears gossip and career discrimination; the client who is afraid of being viewed as weak or disturbed; the client who worries the GP may be disapproving. Counsellors need to weigh up what would be a useful line to take on this matter in general and to make a professional decision based on what is right for the uniqueness of the counselling dyad in question. Simply exploring the issue with the client is often enough for both counsellor and client to come to an understanding of what is right in the particular instance.

Creating a secure framework for counselling

Readers will already know how to set about creating a therapeutic relationship from their work as counsellors. We will not elaborate on this aspect of all counselling relationships but will focus on those areas of counselling which seem to be especially significant in long-term work. Counsellors need to be able to help their clients start the work but they also need to establish boundaries which will protect and safeguard the therapeutic focus of the relationship. The first few counselling sessions create these groundrules for much of what is to follow. Clients do not know where the limits lie in terms of intimacy and formality, in practical terms about times and payment, or what they can feel free to say and do. Regardless of information about such matters, clients will find limits mainly by stumbling across them in the process of counselling. It is the job of the counsellor to attend to everything that is said and done and to respond with the kind of interventions which would be most appropriate to address both the content of the client's personal material and what it may suggest about the process of counselling itself. Tom's counsellor fails to ascertain whether or not he really wants any help or if he is merely accommodating the manager who refers him. Work-related counselling soon gives way to less focused work which opens up pertinent issues for Tom but which he seems to have to endure rather than to explore. The shaky start to counselling does not improve as time goes on, partly perhaps because the inexperienced counsellor cannot pull back from making interventions which are formally correct but for which the client is neither ready nor willing.

It may be the case that the client has been assessed by another counsellor (see Joy, page 36) and the counsellor has the task of picking up issues and feelings which have emerged from the assessment or referral. There may be times when a client has developed a strong transference to the person who has referred them or assessed them. Such a transference may be idealising and get in the way of the therapeutic alliance by stopping the client from moving on to making good use of the counselling available after assessment. Attachment to a safe figure of authority may occur in the face of anxiety about really being able to sustain the intimacy of a counselling relationship and to bring about lasting change. The transference may be more negative, with the client feeling upset about real or imagined slights in being passed on to someone else. Whatever the experience, counsellors of any persuasion will need to listen out for the after-effects of the assessment and to respond in the way which best suits their approach and which helps the client to move into the current relationship.

Counsellors are quite likely to face the setting of boundaries in more literal ways. Payment for sessions in private practice is a good example of a concrete reality which affects the counsellor's work. It is important to mention at the beginning how and when the fee is paid, what happens about missed sessions and holidays and whether or not the fee is negotiable. Exploration around such matters is often fertile ground but tends to emerge over time. It would, in any case, be inappropriate to spend too much time on issues which concern the counsellor more than the client in the early stages of counselling. In non-fee-paying situations, similar issues need to be addressed. Often the client whose motivation is unclear will express this in poor attendance and lateness, as did Tom when he arrived late for his second session. Interestingly, Tom's counsellor seemed to mirror his client's own ambivalence about private counselling in being unable to tackle adequately the question of payment of fees.

The first time the client is late is an opportunity to demonstrate whether or not this will be interpreted, taken as part of the material that is presented and commented on or simply acknowledged. This will establish the kind of focus the client will come to expect. Pamela's concerns (page 28) were initially about her daughter and she seemed to expect the counsellor to help only with this problem. She was late for her first session with the counsellor and perhaps felt disappointed that the GP did not tell her where she could find her daughter. The counsellor responded to what she thought Pamela, in a fragile state of mind, needed most and waited until Pamela was both a more experienced client and had shown she could benefit from more work on herself before offering long-term work. The contract then shifted to more exploratory work where lateness might be interpreted.

Psychodynamic counsellors tend to see the client at the same time and on the same day each week to ensure the client a continuous 'space' which is theirs alone and on which they can come to depend. David (page 48) was quite unstable when he began counselling and benefited from the quiet regularity of his sessions as well as the support he received in them. The counsellor became a fixed reference point for him as he repeated several more swings of mood and periods of disorganisation. Person-centred counsellors may also do this, as did May's counsellor, or they may choose not to encourage such routine in order to avoid inducing a dependent relationship. May's counsellor may even have wished to change a session himself so that it coincided with a painful anniversary, long-term counselling being about caring for another person as well as working with them. Clients often seek to change the time or day of their session and it is up to the counsellor to explore whether this is about a practical necessity or a challenge to the establishment of boundaries. How such matters are tackled will help prepare the client for the kind of commitment and work ahead.

As mentioned earlier, it may be necessary with some clients to establish procedures for crisis situations. Normally if such arrangements are necessary we would expect the counsellor already to have in place a co-operative relationship with any other key workers, as was the case with David. During a hypomanic phase David needed immediate help from his GP and was able to recognise this with the help of the counsellor. Julia's counsellor makes a contract with Julia and her GP – continued loss of weight over a period of time being the barometer to how far the counselling contract could be safely pursued without medical input. There may be agreement for meetings in between sessions for a specific period or for particular reasons or these may be seen as 'frame violations' (Langs, 1994) which damage the counselling contract. The violation of the therapeutic frame would include any rupture of a basic groundrule such as the timing or venue of the counselling session or any other aspect of the contract such as the pledge to keep confidentiality.

Different clients require different responses and the counsellor's setting and theoretical orientation will also determine what is required. Generally, regardless of counsellor orientation, clients who cannot keep to their regular sessions are not suitable to be seen in private practice where there is little administrative or institutional protection from the clients' demands. Once they have settled into a therapeutic relationship, long-term clients may go through periods of more disordered attendance when they touch deeply painful feelings. This is a different matter to clients who are starting out and have not yet settled into the relationship or need other kinds of help. New clients commonly present in a crisis situation and soon become calmed and able to cope, with the support of a counsellor. However, if chaos continues to prevail during the beginning phase of counselling the counsellor may wish to re-assess whether or not the client or the counselling approach is suitable.

Although a contract is made at the beginning of counselling it is never written in stone and may have to be discussed and amended in the light of the day-to-day realities of counselling. In Chapter 3 we saw how counsellors worked with clients for some time before they could decide if a longer term contract was appropriate (see Pamela, page 28; David, page 48; Julia, page 59). One counsellor had to face the consequences of what proved to be a premature move into a longer term contract (see Tom, pages 42–6) and reckon with a wrong decision which not only resulted in a client dropping out of counselling unexpectedly but which also left Tom and his counsellor feeling rather shamed and inadequate. Tom's counsellor could have commented on Tom's lateness in his second session but did not. We would like to suggest that at the beginning of counselling there are, in fact, two contracts with the client: one is spoken and asserted and represents what is desirable in principle; the other is performed over time in day-to day practice. The good counsellor, of any orientation, will bring these two different contracts, which are unavoidably separate at the beginning, closer and closer together so that they become congruent. Tom's counsellor charges for private sessions, including missed ones. However, he is unable to put this into practice in reality so that a modus operandi becomes established whereby Tom does not pay when he misses his appontment and the meaning of his absence is not explored or understood.

Supervision with an experienced colleague who is competent to supervise long-term work is one of the surest ways to secure a solid base on which to carry out long-term counselling and will be discussed more fully in Chapter 6. Starting out with good supervision in place helps the counsellor to keep under review issues which may be of concern and to adjust the approach or the contract at an early point if necessary. It is often through working long-term with difficult clients who are just within the limit of the counsellors' clinical competence that counsellors learn their trade and hone their skills. Joy's counsellor is able to remain helpful to her throughout a stormy period of 'acting out' because her supervisor has explored with the counsellor the way Joy splits people into good and bad. Joy's counsellor may have felt quite assaulted by the strength of Joy's negative feelings, despite understanding them in supervision. Tom's counsellor seems not to have used his supervision to help him make a good assessment of what a client needed and could manage (the two not always being the same). When working with people over time counsellors often feel the need to return to their own personal therapy or to seek out further training. Both of these options may have entered the counsellor's thoughts when Joy was expressing much negativity. Tom's counsellor was perhaps struggling with his own feelings about his personal therapist and acting out some of the tensions in his work with Tom. Where there is a confusion over boundaries, it often has roots which go beyond the client's immediate problem.

Keeping on

This next section tries to give the reader a glimpse of some of the issues which arise when the work is established and proceeding. It is an impossible task in some ways because each client will present a different set of passing problems and underlying dramas. The journey is never the same. There may be either a honeymoon period where the client 'takes' to counselling or getting started may be really hard. If the beginning is straightforward, then the next phase may be more arduous when the 'work' aspect of counselling comes to the fore as client and counsellor struggle to articulate fully feelings and thoughts which begin to influence conscious and unconscious aspects of both parties. This is when the client gets under the counsellor's skin, so to speak, and the maintenance of a solid framework for counselling is tested. Where the start has been rocky, this next phase can sometimes be smoother as some basic issues have already been struggled with or understood. At other times the second phase is as difficult as the first. Beginning counselling often inspires a sense of hope in clients which helps them and counsellors through the early phase when the therapeutic relationship has not strengthened enough to bear the strains of working together towards psychological change.

Ongoing assessment

Pamela is a good example of the second phase of counselling still involving assessment of appropriate goals and interventions. She was offered support in her early experience of counselling while the counsellor gauged if Pamela could benefit from more help when the crisis of her daughter's leaving was over. Next she took on some counselling which was directed at her own experiences as an unsupported mother and was enabled to think about her early childhood deprivations. However, Pamela's counsellor had to measure her interventions against the capacity of her client to withstand thinking about emotional material. If counselling was too painful, Pamela would miss a session. Similarly, the relationship Pamela enjoyed with her counsellor was very difficult for her to think about, especially the contrast it made with her earlier experience of mothering. This difficulty in experiencing a good relationship when childhood deprivation has occurred is related to what Casement calls 'the pain of contrast' (1990: 106). Pamela's counsellor avoided making more interventions from the Cluster 3 end of the scale we mentioned in Chapter 2 because she thought Pamela would be unable to use such forms of counselling intervention. David's counsellor was equally cautious and waited until she could identify the ways in which she could offer help before making a long-term arrangement.

Elton Wilson (1996: 11–28) has formulated a strategy for thinking about commitments that counsellors might make with different clients which employs the idea of three different types of help. She suggests that clients present for help in the first instance in crisis, or to sample counselling, or to start in an informed and appropriate way. After assessment there will follow a short 'holding' period or a 'mini-commitment'. After this point the engagement may end or there might be a referral elsewhere. If help continues she identifies three kinds: time-focused (10–13 sessions); time-expanded (12+ sessions with a final date for ending already set); and time-extended (with 2 months notice of an agreed ending, up to 5 years duration and regular reviews). We welcome this clear way of thinking about how counselling may unfold.

For Pamela, there was a 'holding' and then a period of time-expanded counselling, followed by more open-ended work. Review was not carried out in a formal way but at each ebb in the flow of the work the counsellor was able to think about the commitment with Pamela and whether or not to continue. A similar pattern emerged in David's counselling. Both cases demonstrate that in our schema one kind of commitment might lead into another rather than exclude the other options. It is in this subtle way that reviews often take place in counselling and contracts are reaffirmed or changed. However, some counsellors do prefer to plan and carry out periodic reviews more formally to gauge how the work is being perceived by the client.

Goals

Closely allied to the notion of commitment and contract is the question of goals. These tend to shift in counselling as the client moves from one perspective on themselves and their difficulties to another. Tom's counsellor misunderstood that his client's agreement to go on working together was not an informed or committed choice. The counsellor's intentions to proceed with the work, though coloured by his own needs, were relevant in terms of the material Tom produced about his life, which could have been worked on in counselling. However, goals need to be agreed in practice as well as in words. Where money exchanges hands, the mind can be focused concretely on whether or not counselling feels valuable to the client. Where there is no fee, the client can feel swept along by the counsellor's good intentions or by gratitude for the help that has already been given. Counsellors should be able to explain the goals they are working towards though clients may conceive of them in very general terms.

Julia's counsellor, for example, could easily identify that she was aiming to help Julia cease to starve herself and learn to enjoy her body and her life. These goals were, however, quite ambitious and the counsellor set steps along the way to this ideal resolution. This meant that, in the early phase of counselling, the goal was to help Julia form a counselling relationship and to stop losing weight. The middle phase was about exploring the underlying feelings which led to Julia adopting such a severe attitude to her own needs. During this middle part of Julia's journey of self-discovery she made a new relationship and opted to start a new phase of her life elsewhere. This is not uncommon in Julia's age group. Counselling is only one of the ways in which people change their lives and though we might expect Julia to continue to experience some problems of self-worth and of body image, she may seek further help at a later stage or find her own solutions in due course.

The developing relationship

Julia's blossoming attachment is soon transferred to a boyfriend. However, many clients form the closest attachment they have ever experienced as adults to their counsellor. The intensity of such bonds can be tremendous: in May's case, her counsellor becomes a lifeline at a time when her grief is unbearable both for herself and her family and friends. The counsellor must survive both positive and negative transference as well as cope with the pressure of giving someone attention and care over a long period of time. Counsellors usually have an Achilles' heel about some aspect of their work, but for long-term counsellors there must be a capacity to support a lengthening attachment and the dependency which often accompanies it without becoming anxious. May's counsellor felt relaxed about the attachment but needed to consider very carefully the practical requirements of making sure he could continue to see her when there were other demands on him.

The practical aspects of a long-term commitment include planning ahead for holiday breaks so that clients do not have to adapt too hurriedly to a change of routine or do without the support of a counsellor at a particularly difficult time. The middle part of May's counselling was very painful and she sometimes seemed to be on the edge of a pathological grief reaction. She needed a faithful counsellor who would stay with her as she grieved and who could cope with the depth of pain she kept trying to deny. At times she was quite flirtatious, as if a replacement for her husband would have helped her block out the pain. Her counsellor was able to feel affection and attraction without mistaking his role for a less professional one. Following her shifts of mood and increasing ability to tolerate feelings led the counsellor into experiences which were disturbing for him as, for example, when she hallucinated her husband's presence in the session.

Breaks

Any absence on the part of the client or the counsellor will merit special attention in a long-term counselling relationship. Sometimes absences are experienced as abandonments, as might have ocurred with Pamela if she had been less well defended, or as potential losses, as May often felt. Joy's counselling shifted focus when she experienced a flooding back of memories of abuse. The counsellor adjusted to the changes made by Joy's disclosure and responded to the accompanying shift in transference which came shortly after when a break occurred, causing Joy to feel as if she could not really count on her counsellor for support at a critical time. Rage ensued and the counselling relationship almost broke down. Joy's counsellor was helped to look at how, in the countertransference, she had enjoyed the positive transference and had unwittingly colluded with the splitting of ambivalent feelings about people into good and bad. This was a learning opportunity for counsellor and client.

Pamela, on the other hand, found holiday breaks and cancellations so painful and redolent of her childhood abandonments that she could not consciously let herself be aware of them. The counsellor carefully assessed how much she could address of this early trauma and how much she must leave alone. Obviously, sometimes a client is justifiably pleased to have coped without the counsellor during a long break but there are also times when coping without the counsellor represents a denial of missing someone rather than coping with loss. Clients may cancel sessions before a break or after it as a way of convincing themselves that they do not need the counsellor. When such behaviour replaces talking about such matters in counselling, the counsellor is faced with acting out behaviour: a form of communication that needs to be understood with the client.

Monitoring the work

As counselling gets under way there will probably emerge 'natural breaks' when a review of how the work is progressing will seem to arise spontaneously. Planning for the summer break, which for most counsellors is the longest, will offer both client and counsellor an opportunity to think about the duration of their work together. Often clients who are afraid of dependency will return after a break and suggest that they end soon. Sometimes, of course, a break gives the client a genuine opportunity to practise being on their own in the world. Unlike short or medium-term work, long-term counselling is modulated, like most of our lives, by the rhythms of the world around us. Keeping an eye on changes taking place or not in the everyday life of the client outside the counselling room will also help the counsellor to monitor the client's progress. We need to explore situations as they arise to make sure that a client is really ready for ending rather than inviting a premature break in fear of outstaying their welcome.

Maintaining an open mind

One danger of long-term counselling is that the counsellor may become blinkered, fall into a habitual way of hearing and relating to the client and hence miss important communications because they are new and unfamiliar. This might be especially likely in those counsellors with a heavy case load which includes both short- and long-term work. The sessions with long-term clients may come as something of a relief after the pressures of continually assessing and familiarising oneself with new histories and patterns of relating which short-term work demands. It may then become difficult to maintain the helpful distance which is so necessary in a counselling relationship, the ability to observe and reflect on the counselling process at the same time as being fully present for the client. The counsellor needs to hold on to curiosity and the freedom to make imaginative leaps in order to sidestep or break established unhelpful patterns.

There is a possibility of collusion in avoiding difficult areas. For example, the counsellors of Anna and Joy both very much enjoyed their clients and the positive feeling between them but at times they lost their perspective and hence an awareness of the more negative feelings their clients might experience. Luckily their supervisors were able to point out their blind spots. Sometimes a dream or events in an outside relationship will alert counsellor and client to something that needs to be explored between them but is being kept outside. One client who came religiously for every session and professed no dissatisfaction with her counsellor began to have a series of quite violent dreams which revealed a normally unexpressed aspect of herself. Another claimed the counselling was very helpful but persisted in her involvement with an abusive partner. In both cases an exploration of what was being avoided between counsellor and client allowed the work to progress.

Trusting the process

It is not at all uncommon for counsellors, however experienced, to be puzzled about the significance of clients' communications within a particular session or over a period of time or to feel overwhelmed by the force of feeling they encounter. Counsellors new to long-term work may be troubled by this, particularly if they are not very advanced in their own therapy. We would suggest that it is important to learn to stay with the uncertainty of not knowing, to avoid leaping to premature conclusions in order to escape the anxiety associated with feeling confused and unable to offer any immediate relief for the client's painful feelings. This is not to advocate a passive waiting for the dawning of enlightenment but a willingness to stay with and reflect on the experience of being with the client. This can sometimes be so powerful that counsellors can seem to forget what they know, but such forgetting can be an important factor in trying to understand the process.

Perhaps the most important thing for new counsellors to remember is how important they are to all their clients, but perhaps especially to those they see long-term. They have of course read about this and been taught it but grasping this understanding emotionally as well as theoretically can take a great deal of time. It can seem grandiose to assert one's importance to someone else but it is crucial to understand your significance to the client not as yourself but as a person in a role within the counselling relationship. Attending to the quality of this relationship and the way it is shifting (whether these are commented on or not) is always helpful. Often it is the supervisor who, being more experienced and less immediately involved, can shed most light on the nature of the relationship which is being established and changes on it.

Attention to one's own feelings is also essential. Some clients have great difficulty in tolerating certain feelings and may project them into their counsellors in an effort both to rid themselves of discomfort and to convey important information about themselves. We gave an example of this in Chapter 4 on assessment when we discussed the young man who initially aroused a powerful wish to rescue him in the counsellor. Again it can feel pretentious to pay so much attention to one's own responses but these can yield invaluable information so long as the counsellor has enough self-knowledge to distinguish personal from client material.

The sequence of communications within a session and in a series of sessions and their timing in relation to breaks are always worth listening for. Careful observation of the beginning and end of sessions and of clients' reactions to the counsellor's interventions is useful. Counsellors do need to be open to the possibility that they have reached the limits of their ability and not just muddle on, hoping for the best. But they also need a willingness to trust the process and to persevere. Long-term counselling affords the opportunity for convincing change if counsellors have the patience to wait, the readiness to let themselves be used and the capacity to be honest about uncertainties with themselves and in supervision.

Difficulties and impasses

We have in mind situations in counselling which everyone will at some time encounter: serious ones where the counselling seems to be about to break down; where the counselling seems to be drifting to a close; and less serious ones where the counselling becomes temporarily disrupted. The countertransference aspects of such experiences are discussed in Chapter 6.

Where a client becomes violent and aggressive or too disturbed to work with the counsellor is an extreme example. The more common situation is where there is a shift away from counselling which cannot be addressed. David was a very disturbed young man whose dramatic hypomanic crises alternated with a very low-key kind of depression. He was able to use counselling both to keep himself from harm and to explore some of the life circumstances such as passing exams, getting a decent place to live and making friends. His counsellor could sense many deep-seated problems in his family relationships and his personality but could not envisage how David could develop any insight about them. His description of a trapdoor that he could not get open but behind which were many feelings was a perfect image of the situation also experienced by the counsellor. She was faced with a counselling client who could not explore beyond the fringes of his awareness without losing the precious stability she had helped him to re-establish. Although she felt very fond of him their time together also seemed a waste of resources and she began to feel bored. Sleepiness and boredom are not uncommon experiences for counsellors in long-term work, though they have been associated in psychoanalytic therapy with countertransference reactions to people with borderline personalities and should therefore invite some self-reflection when detected. Psychodynamic counsellors may wonder what is being communicated to them when such states become conscious. There is a growing body of literature on drowsiness in psychotherapy which counsellors may wish to read (see Brown, 1977; Wangh, 1979; Shamni, 1985). Similarly, person-centred counsellors will want to explore the meaning of this non-accepting attitude which is induced in them. Counsellors do also get jaded and this is discussed in the next chapter.

However, the eventual disappearance of David into the mass of the student body represented a great step forward for him – he just became an unremarkable student who had better things to do with his time than see a counsellor. This impasse was eventually resolved by David missing sessions and leaving in a casual way. Perhaps the counsellor could have taken the initiative in ending the counselling but that would have been more like David being sent away rather than leaving home and may have conveyed a wish for him to be more dramatic if he were to continue. Her letter meant that he could return if he wished.

Tom's counselling reaches a similar impasse, though for different reasons, and is, overall more of a failure than the success that David has earned. Tom's counsellor seems to make mistakes all along the line and cannot learn from them in supervision. The counselling collapses without Tom's counsellor helping both of them face the problems they had in working together. Perhaps a more experienced counsellor would be able to recognise mistakes and take reparative action earlier. We all have blind spots in our counselling work which is why we value the impartial view of a supervisor to help us glimpse what we cannot see ourselves.

Joy's counselling goes through a difficult period when she discloses to her grandmother that she has been abused and is told that it was all in the past and of no great consequence. The therapeutic relationship becomes home to all the rage and betrayal that Joy has been repressing for years and the counsellor is made to feel that she is no good and must be punished. Missed sessions and threats to leave are part of working through this difficult experience for Joy. The therapeutic relationship is strained but not destroyed.

Letters, phonecalls and visits from family and friends

When counsellors work long-term with clients they are more likely to make an impact on the significant people in the client's world through the work they are doing. Partners and friends may feel jealous, possessive, threatened, guilty: the range of possible feelings is extensive. It is up to each counsellor to evaluate the meaning and consequences of any encounter with a person who is connected to the client in some way. David's father and his friend both contacted the counsellor. In this case the counsellor respected the need for both parties to have their say but did not discuss David's counselling with them. She would not be drawn into collusion with either, nor did she reject either's approach. In this example both people told David their plans and David told the counsellor he wanted the contacts to go ahead. Not every approach to a counsellor will be as straightforward as these two cases. The counsellor's attitude to such matters will be affected by the setting and the counsellor's own orientation and personal style. In student counselling services it is not uncommon for parents to express concern about their grown-up children and they are often managed as clients in their own right, without confidentiality being broken. Similarly, in such settings young people often feel as if they are like a family to other students with whom they live and will approach the counselling service for advice. Sometimes the 'caretaker' is the person who most needs counselling though it is not advisable that the long-term counsellor be the person to take on this task.

Endings

*What particular issues are likely to arise when ending
long-term counselling?*

Some of the concerns here will be the same as in any counselling. Perhaps the ending of long-term work may be more poignant because of the sense of timelessness and implicit promise of perfect resolution (in which both counsellor and client may have their separate or joint investments) that may characterise long-term work and pervade the relationship. The ending points both counsellor and client back to 'real' time and to the fact of other more permanent relationships. It signifies the reality – which both may find bruising – that, however close, this has been a professional relationship.

As with all counselling it is always preferable to agree the ending date in advance and not to change it lightly. An important part of making a contract for open-ended counselling is a discussion of how its eventual ending will be decided. It may be difficult for inexperienced counsellors to realise how dependent their clients may become and how betrayed they may feel if their counsellors raise the issue of ending prematurely or underplay its significance. Having time to work on the ending is vital: it enables the counselling couple to reflect on their joint work and relationship and their significance; it focuses the attention on loss, an area of universal concern; and it allows for some shared anticipation of the future. The counsellor might find it helpful to review case notes in the closing period of long-term work; this may prompt thinking about what has changed and alert attention to themes likely to be replayed at this stage. It is always more satisfactory to have a planned ending but it is particularly difficult in long-term work if either counsellor or client breaks off prematurely.

What to do if the counsellor has to end prematurely?

In the next chapter we will discuss the need for forward planning so that counsellors do not commit themselves to long-term work which they know they will be unable to complete. However, the unexpected does happen. Work may have to be given up for unforeseen reasons due to an upheaval in the counsellor's personal circumstances such as a change in job or serious personal or family illness.

If the counsellor is breaking the agreement he or she has to consider how much to offer explanations or reassurance and how much to leave space for clients to express and explore their own reactions and understandings about being left unexpectedly. Gray (1994), writing from within the psychodynamic framework, provides an interesting discussion of an early ending brought about by her leaving an agency where she chose not to give the client much information in order to allow her the opportunity to consider different possible meanings for herself. A person-centred counsellor might be inclined for the sake of mutuality to give more explanation for her reasons for changing an agreement about the length of counselling but would still be most concerned with the client's response.

Matters are even more difficult if a counsellor has to end abruptly or take a long break unexpectedly because of some private tragedy. In such cases we feel that the client needs to be told that the counsellor's decision is neither arbitrary nor impulsive; perhaps counsellors can indicate the serious, personal and unexpected nature of the circumstances without burdening clients or themselves with detailed explanations. At the very least there needs to be a letter for the client and if at all possible a meeting. Hard though it may be for counsellors preoccupied with their own difficulties, they should be open to the range of feelings which clients may have about the disruption, including those of concern for the counsellor.

In some cases when the counsellor has to end the work early a referral may be desirable. Then the counsellor has to maintain a delicate balance, acknowledging both the need for the client to continue with counselling and the competency of other practitioners and the particularity and significance of the relationship that is coming to an end.

All counsellors and especially those in private practice need to have prepared for the eventuality of serious accident or death (Traynor and Clarkson, 1992). Someone reliable, preferably a professional colleague rather than a partner, must know how to find addresses and telephone numbers for clients so that they can be sensitively informed. This needs to be discussed in advance with a colleague or supervisor who will agree to contact and refer clients if necessary.

What if the client ends prematurely?
A more usual scenario is when a client breaks off the work while it is still incomplete as did our imaginary clients, Tom, David and

Julia. Tom's ending was the most abrupt. The counsellor wrote to Tom after his second non-appearance, saying merely that he realised things had been difficult, was sorry Tom had not kept his appointments and that he was keeping them free. Tom did not reply and did not show up. The counsellor then wrote again, a more interpretative letter this time, explaining how he saw some of the difficulties and inviting Tom to come for at least one session to talk these through. Again Tom did not reply. The counsellor wrote acknowledging the fact and saying he assumed Tom was not wishing to continue for the time being; he could contact the counsellor again in the future if he wished to. The supervisor had warned the counsellor against a more effusive invitation, pointing out that if Tom did return the counsellor would have to do a proper assessment and perhaps refer him elsewhere – he should not commit himself blindly to long-term work at any time in the future Tom might wish. The counsellor enclosed his bill which, even at a second prompting, Tom ignored.

David's ending was rather different. He seemed to detach himself over a period of time; for a while he came fortnightly rather than weekly, then he began to miss sessions and finally vanished altogether. His counsellor had already decided not to push him into too much exploration as she feared this might upset the rather fragile equilibrium he had managed to achieve. Hence she refrained from writing to him in any interpretative way but did make sure he knew that she was still available to him. Her decision to do this was based on her understanding of David's difficulties, rather than her routine response to any client who discontinued counselling without warning.

The sudden departure of any client who has agreed to long-term counselling should make the counsellor reflect on what might be the reasons. Was the initial assessment and choice of type of counselling faulty? Could some other current or earlier relationship be being acted out with the counsellor? Has the counsellor been clumsy, unfeeling or unhearing? Is the process just too painful or potentially painful for the client at the moment? Is it simply not what the client expected or wants?

We think it important to acknowledge all absences and to invite clients back so that their meaning and the feelings around them can be worked on. At the same time it is important not to harass clients who have the right to make their own decisions and have them respected.

Other clients may not disappear, as Tom and David did, but instead come to their sessions announcing they feel much better while failing to convince their counsellors that they have really dealt with their difficulties – a syndrome often described as a flight into health. Pamela's presentation to the counsellor when her daughter first returned home was like this although she did respond to the counsellor's gentle suggestion about continuing. Again counsellors need to take time to explore the possible meanings of sudden cures but must ultimately accept clients' decisions.

How to decide an ending date?

Sometimes a change in a client's external circumstances – which may be due in part to successful counselling work – may prompt a consideration of ending. Julia is an instance of this; her counselling has contributed to her growing self-confidence, ability to form relationships and have more ambition for herself. A new job, a move or a graduation will be known about some time in advance and may provide the spur to review the work and decide that enough has been done. The linking of ending counselling with a life event can mean that the client finds it difficult to focus on the loss involved and so misses a valuable therapeutic opportunity. We would suggest it is better to avoid an exact coincidence of timing unless, as in some grief counselling, the timing of an ending is being deliberately manipulated to help the client face a difficult issue. For example, long-term work with students might end either well before or after final examinations, allowing them to concentrate on each fully. Ending should not coincide with the anniversary of a bereavement or other important loss.

A more difficult circumstance is when an impasse has been reached and no therapeutic progress is discernible. Many clients with this perception will stop coming but others may persist: perhaps because they cannot face the disappointment and loss of hope involved in leaving; perhaps because they are masochistic or overly submissive; perhaps because they are replaying some drama from their past. It can be difficult for counsellors too to acknowledge that no productive work is taking place. This can feel like giving up on the client or admitting defeat and failure. Sometimes clients do react negatively to the therapeutic process and make no progress, however much help they are offered.

We are definitely not advocating that the first or even second reaction to a period of lost direction in the work should be to suggest ending. An impasse needs to be thought about and discussed with both the client and one's supervisor. There are, however, occasions when the most ethical course of action may be to accept one's own limitations or those of a particular counsellor/client match and to suggest ending. It may be appropriate in such cases to refer to someone more experienced or to acknowledge that the client is free to seek further help in the future.

Perhaps the most common reason for ending any counselling, including long-term, is when enough has been done for the time being. This would be true of both May and Joy. May has made considerable progress at coming to terms with her loss and is able to take up her own life again. Joy has come to understand the reasons for her depression and has taken control of her life. Both counsellors felt satisfied with their work.

Pamela's counsellor had more unease about the ending as she was aware of many areas of difficulty which her client had not been able to face. However, she accepted that enough had been done for Pamela to feel more comfortable with herself. Some people can accept limited goals for themselves. Many may want to take a rest from counselling and have the option of re-engaging with the process later, if not with the same counsellor, although these attitudes may be quite difficult for a new and enthusiastic counsellor to accept. Perhaps we need to beware of misplaced therapeutic perfectionism. As Walker puts it succinctly, 'the client is striving towards a sufficient resolution, not a perfect solution' (1992: 169). Counsellors need to acknowledge that people do develop outside therapeutic relationships and, as Elton Wilson (1996) argues, may benefit from working with different practitioners and in different ways at different stages in their development.

In arguing for good enough progress as a reason for ending, we are not advocating defeatism, nor an undervaluing of what can be achieved. We are suggesting that the best can sometimes be the enemy of the good and lead counsellors to feel and perhaps to convey to their clients an unnecessary sense of dissatisfaction with good progress because it falls short of perfection.

Who should decide?
Preferably the decision to end counselling should be mutual. Discussion may be initiated by either client or counsellor. When the client raises the issue, the counsellor needs to listen extra carefully to what is being said and the feelings and thoughts that

may be implicit in the suggestion which might, for example, contain a disguised reproach about some recent development in the counselling (as was the case with Joy); a fear that the client is a burden to the counsellor; an attempt to replay past experiences of rejection; or a concern that the counsellor may resent the client's striving for autonomy. It is important not to make a precipitate response but to allow plenty of time for exploring the meanings of the client's desire to leave. If the counsellor is the one to raise the issue he or she needs to think very carefully about the best way to word it and to be especially alert to the client's response.

How long should be allowed for ending?
Some would argue that the issues raised during the termination period are so crucial that a third of all the time available for counselling should be devoted to ending. A substantial proportion of the time with May and Joy was spent on ending. Elton Wilson (1996) argues that long-term work requires at least two months' notice of ending to allow for all the issues to be worked with and makes an explicit agreement with the client about this at the outset. We think this is probably a safe minimum to work with but recognise that the period necessary for dealing with ending will vary according to the length of the counselling, individual clients and the nature of their difficulties.

When to change a previously agreed date?
Once a date for ending has been set it is normally best to keep to it but there are occasions such as the client's developing a serious illness or encountering unpredicted changes of circumstance when some alteration might be negotiated. The emergence of new material in the counselling sessions at this stage is not unusual but is often best dealt with by looking at the fear of ending or wish for total resolution which may have been the motive for its expression.

What issues are likely to arise in this phase?
Malan (1995) points out that in long-term work many of the issues we might expect around termination will have been foreshadowed in working on feelings about breaks so final termination may be less of an issue than in more focused work. It may be that endings are relatively straightforward, that clients' predominant feelings are of pleasure at progress made and gratitude for the help they have received.

However, Molnos (1995), also an advocate of brief therapy in many cases, suggests that the work of a long-term engagement is likely to intensify with the setting of a termination date. It is probable that there will be some painful feelings – probably on both sides – about the ending. Any ending is likely to resurrect past losses and the grief and conflicts associated with them. This consideration was uppermost in the mind of May's counsellor as they worked towards ending.

It may be that even clients who have completed counselling fairly successfully will have a sense of disappointment and dis-illusion that not all their hopes have been realised. As Mearns and Thorne point out:

> While they are pleased with the new self which has emerged, there may also be a tinge of disappointment that their successful progress through counselling does not mean that life is easy hereafter. Sometimes the client has built up a fairy-tale image of what life would be like 'if only I were well'. Such a fairy-tale ending, with its theme of 'living happily ever after', does not bear much resemblance to the reality of having to construct a new life to fit the self which has emerged. (Mearns and Thorne, 1988: 142)

Sometimes an agreement to end may prove the trigger to the reappearance of the client's greatest difficulties. One author recalls working with someone who experienced the setting of an ending date, albeit a year in advance, as an affront similar to the one he felt was inflicted by his mother's having another child after him. There followed six months of total resentment and rage, non-co-operation and threatened self-destructive behaviour before any progress was resumed. This was an extreme reaction to ending but many clients do have a sense of being left for someone else – perhaps a member of the counsellor's family or a more needy successor. This is a theme well worth listening for.

We would suggest that most clients feel a certain amount of ambivalence about ending and that it is vital for the counsellor to acknowledge their mixed feelings. Relief is one feeling that is often missed; counselling can be very hard work for the client who engages fully. Anger is often present and needs to be openly expressed. Another feeling sometimes dodged by counsellors is gratitude; it may be embarrassing for the counsellor to accept thanks but it is important to do so. Presents are more difficult; some counsellors feel they need to be interpreted; others that a gracious acceptance is all that is called for. We think this is a time for lightness of touch and gentle reference if any to the meaning of a gift.

What might the counsellor's own feelings be?
Like clients, counsellors are likely to have mixed feelings about ending. Indeed it would be very worrying if counsellors were to greet the end of any long-term counselling involvement with total equanimity. They may experience sadness, pleasure, possibly relief, possibly gratitude for an experience shared and learning gained, possibly guilt about not having helped more, curiosity about the client's future, maybe feelings about any other practitioner the client may work with in the future. While the emphasis must stay on exploring the client's experience, we think most counsellors will want to acknowledge the importance of the work for them and their own sense of loss at the ending. Person-centred practitioners may choose to be rather more self-revelatory than psychodynamic ones. We would suggest that it is possible and necessary to be personal and genuine while holding on to the boundaries of the counselling role.

Is the ending really final?
There are many choices to be made at the end of long-term counselling. Some counsellors, like Pamela's in our case example, always or sometimes tell clients that their door is always open should the client feel the need for further consultation. Some arrange a follow-up meeting some months after the ending. Some explicitly draw clients' attention to the possibility of future work with someone else or of negotiating a new contract with themselves. Others may make no such offers but would still be ready to respond should former clients approach them. We would suggest choosing from these options in the light of what is judged likely to be most helpful to individual clients. Offering the opportunity for further contact may blunt the impact of ending and the need to take stock of work done or not done for some clients yet provide a necessary softening and recognition of the potential for future development for others.

Sometimes counsellors may wish to contact clients. This may be because they want to follow up the work for research purposes or because they wish to publish case material based on the counselling. Clearly counsellors need to think through the implications and wisdom of such departures from the normal frame of the work. If they decide to proceed they need to be sensitive to any reluctance on the part of the client and the complexities of truly informed consent and provide the opportunity to discuss without pressure the implications of the research or writing. They may judge it would be too upsetting, exciting or intrusive to contact certain former clients, but in that case will have to forgo using them as examples. No one should be exposed to the shock of stumbling upon a case study of themselves for which they have not given permission.

Sometimes clients return or write a long time after the conclusion of counselling. This can be one of the pleasures of long-term involvement in that it provides the opportunity for both parties to acknowledge the importance of the relationship, satisfies the counsellor's natural curiosity and allows for some mutual assessment of the durability of the work. Sometimes of course clients return because they are in trouble, perhaps for a one-off session, perhaps for further work or referral. Return visits might be more problematic if they are indicators of unresolved and unrecognised difficulties in the counselling relationship, a possibility to be alert for.

Often there will be unplanned encounters between former counsellors and clients. This is especially likely in smaller communities, within minority groups and where there are professional links. Counsellors may need to consider with the client before ending the possibility and management of such encounters. Mearns and Thorne (1988) address the questions involved when engaging in a different kind of relationship with former clients from a person-centred viewpoint, arguing that former clients can become friends and colleagues with little difficulty but cautioning against sexual relationships. A psychodynamic viewpoint would be much more conservative and would stress the inadvisability of forming social relationships with former clients because of the emphasis in that tradition on the power of the transference. Whatever stance counsellors choose, they should take account of the different needs of each client and monitor the effects of their decision in practice.

6

Practical and Emotional Issues for the Counsellor

Chapter 4 concerned the assessment of clients' suitability and readiness for long-term work. This chapter is about the counsellor's self-assessment of his or her own suitability to undertake this kind of counselling commitment and approach. As our introduction indicated, long-term counselling is not without its risks for both client and counsellor. We hope this chapter will help counsellors to make informed judgements about their practical and emotional readiness to do this kind of work – at all or with particular clients. The chapter is structured as a series of questions under which we discuss issues of formal preparation, support, personal qualities, motivations and rewards in this kind of work. We introduce ways of thinking about and responding to individual clients and possible ways forward if, despite the exercise of care at the outset, things seem to be going wrong.

Am I properly prepared? Have I sufficient theoretical and experiential understanding?

These questions raise issues of training, institutional and personal authority. Our introduction indicated ongoing debates and concerns about professional legitimacy. Although there is no legal bar to stop anyone offering long-term or any other form of counselling, there are many professional and ethical considerations. In practice counsellors do not usually decide alone whether or not to take on new clients. They will refer to the views of their supervisors and in some cases medical opinion and – if not in private practice – to organisational policy. We would recommend that counsellors attend to these, seek accreditation and registration and reflect on their own motivations and capabilities.

Training

What kind of training might be appropriate? Most counselling trainings prepare their students for general counselling and do not concentrate exclusively on preparation for long-term counselling or make it a condition of qualification to have worked with clients on this basis. However, many advanced diploma and masters courses have the expectation that their students will do some longer work and produce at least one case study of an extended piece of counselling, which will demonstrate their capacity to hold clients over time. Some would argue that good short-term work can be done only by those with a grounding in the experience of long-term. Many of the WPF counselling courses do focus on preparing for long-term work and require trainees to undertake it. The BAC and COSCA accreditation schemes – the main routes to registration for independent counsellors in the UK – do require counsellors to have completed a certain number of hours of supervised practice over a period of years. They do not specify that these should include some long-term contact but do ask for case study evidence.

The number of counselling courses on offer is expanding. They vary in length, depth, orientation and degree of specialisation and those embarking on a course may wish to consider carefully whether what is on offer meets their needs and interests. A longer course – and many now last for three years – which gives time for the study of the issues raised in long-term counselling would be more suitable for someone interested in this kind of work. Counsellors from many orientations undertake long-term work and would suggest that their approaches are suitable preparations. Elton Wilson (1996: 135) argues that features of both the person-centred and psychodynamic approaches are necessary for this kind of work (she describes it as 'time-expanded') and suggests that practitioners should draw particularly on 'the more empathic and non-defensive transformations of psychoanalytic theory and methodology'. She makes particular reference to Kahn (1991) who emphasises the work of Kohut and Rogers.

Another consideration is the kind of counselling experience necessary for or provided by a course. Many trainees will have a counselling element to their jobs and will be able to take that for supervision on their courses, but others have to find a suitable placement. Some courses are in a better position to facilitate placements than others and some placements are more able to provide experience with long-term clients. We would advocate that novice counsellors get their initial experience in established services or agencies which can provide adequate accommodation, skilled reception and good supervision. If counselling is provided as one facility within a larger organisation, the institutional parameters should have been clearly thought through and the relationship of counselling with other institutional tasks clarified. The new counsellor is then free to concentrate on the dynamics in the counselling room without the worry of negotiating with other parts of an organisation about the legitimacy of the work.

Because we think that the kind of holding and support provided by an established setting can be so helpful, we do not consider situations where a learner is the only counsellor or private practice suitable for new or inexperienced counsellors. It can be hard to obtain decently paid counselling work and frustrating not to be able to use the skills and enthusiasm gained from a course, but many practitioners would suggest that new graduates should exercise caution about – or refrain altogether from – moving immediately into private practice or work in poorly conceived (and poorly paid) posts as these situations can be detrimental to the development of counsellor and client alike. The enthusiasm brought by novice counsellors often leads to excellent work, but it does need to be balanced by the understanding and experience of longer qualified practitioners and institutional support.

Personal counselling or therapy

We are convinced of the importance of therapy and counselling for those wanting to undertake long-term work with clients and think counselling trainings should strongly encourage (as many do) their students to have the experience of working on their personal histories and difficulties by being clients themselves. This view is supported by BAC's new requirement that from 1998 counsellors must have a minimum of 40 hours personal counselling or equivalent actively consistent with the counsellor's core model to

be considered for accreditation. Counsellors from different orientations support the desirability of practitioners working on their own
issues. Noonan, coming from the psychoanalytic tradition, argues:

> The most effective and appropriate training however is personal
> therapy or counselling. Nowhere else is there the opportunity to focus
> on personal dynamics, feelings and intentions. The counsellor's own
> emotional resources are her greatest ally in her work, so if she is
> ignorant of them, afraid of them or unable to rely on them, she is
> severely handicapped – and she handicaps her clients. (Noonan, 1983:
> 129)

Mearns and Thorne argue that 'work on the self can never be
complete' (1988: 37–8) and suggest:

> The person-centred counsellor does well to participate in a group
> where it is possible to articulate feelings of inadequacy, incompetence,
> hopelessness and shame in the knowledge that such feelings will be
> respected and understood, and will not be taken as signs of weakness
> or professional uselessness. (Mearns and Thorne, 1988: 26)

Dryden et al. point to the lack of research evidence for the relationship between counsellors' personal therapy and their efficacy
with clients. They question whether personal therapy alone can
guarantee all that is necessary for trainee counsellor's self-
development but nonetheless conclude:

> although it is an expensive addition to training, on-going personal
> therapy provides great personal support and also a context in which
> students can explore the roots of any personal issues arising during
> training and work with clients. The focused individual attention offered
> by personal therapy can reach depths which are not easily attained in
> other training contexts and may well contribute, albeit indirectly, to
> clinical effectiveness as a counsellor. (Dryden et al., 1995: 100–1)

One of our respondents commented: 'I enjoy long-term work
because I am helping, or trying to help, people who, like myself,
carry a heavy load of emotional damage.' People are often
attracted to the work because of their own personal histories and a
good experience of working these through in therapy can only
enhance their sensitivity to clients. Nonetheless it is vital to be able
to distinguish oneself from the client; Tom's counsellor's enthusiasm for his own therapy blinded him to Tom's very different
views. Our examples of the work with Joy and Pamela illustrate
how their counsellors' self-awareness, developed through personal therapy, alerted them to some of their clients' patterns and

helped them avoid contributing to these in an unhelpful and unquestioning way.

We think that the kind of learning that can occur in personal therapeutic exploration chosen out of a sense of one's own need, not merely to satisfy an external requirement, is necessary for the counsellor contemplating long-term work. We would recommend that counsellors do not offer a much longer engagement or one of much greater frequency than they themselves have experienced as clients.

Personal therapy, like every other aspect of preparation for the work, needs to be digested so that it is in the background when with the client. Immersion in and excitement about their own therapy should not blind counsellors to the need to moderate their approach and expectations to suit different clients, the setting and the length and frequency of meetings. Tom's counsellor was very concerned with dealing with his relationship with his father in his own therapy and so rather overemphasised the importance of Tom's relationship with his father while not attending enough to other important parts of Tom's history and feelings about himself. We might compare this with Pamela's rather more experienced counsellor who had worked a lot on her relationship with her own mother and so was able to avoid being over-identified with Pamela and to see her more clearly.

Do I have the requisite immediate support?

Supervision

All good trainings require students to have a good deal of supervision, but the need for supervision does not end with graduation from a course. Bramley argues that 'it is as unethical and irresponsible as it is dangerous to meddle in someone's deeply private feelings, hurts, memories and thoughts without adequate recourse to the second opinion of a more experienced practitioner' (1996a: 34). Indeed, the BAC Code of Ethics for Counsellors requires its members who are practising counsellors to have ongoing supervision throughout their careers. A good working relationship with a supervisor is one of the most important tools that counsellors have for supporting and reviewing their work with clients. The judgement of a supervisor who has considerable experience of undertaking and supervising long-term work and who knows the counsellor's work well will be very helpful to people considering taking on long-term clients, particularly when they have little previous experience. One respondent to our letter in *Counselling* wrote:

> I think long-term work is the counselling form where supervision is most essential, because the longer the work with one client, the more likely I am to get drawn into transference/countertransference issues which I haven't recognised, and the more I will need the space for reflection and exploration with my supervisor.

Supervision is the subject of an increasing number of courses, much current discussion and a growing literature. For further discussion of the use that counsellors might make of supervisors, see Dryden and Thorne (1991), Feltham and Dryden (1994), Bramley (1996b), Jacobs (1996) and Shipton (1997).

Institutional authority

Counselling is of course about deeply personal and private issues as explored in a relationship between two people. However, it always takes place in a setting which will have a real and phantasised influence on the work. Counsellors need to be clear that they have the institutional authority to undertake this kind of work. An agency or organisation may put limits on the length of contract or areas of exploration, usually because of limited resources. This can be frustrating for both the counsellor and client who have discovered a mutual wish to do long-term work. Indeed Mearns and Thorne argue:

> person-centred counsellors will find it difficult to work in agencies where policy dictates that clients can have a certain number of sessions and no more. Such a system takes away power from both counsellor and client, and it is only by acknowledging, accepting and transcending such shared impotence that a person-centred counsellor and her client could work constructively together. (Mearns and Thorne, 1988: 110–11)

Nonetheless counsellors would be ill-advised to get involved in offering long-term contracts in defiance of organisational policy. It is not helpful for the client to be invited to collude with the counsellor in disregarding authority; moreover there is a risk of the work being interrupted unless it has the clear mandate of the agency. Regrettably many counsellors in education are now employed on casual term-time only contracts which must be renewed (or not) each academic year. In this situation it is probably fairer to the client to offer only time-limited work although, given the extensive difficulties many students face, this will not always be ideal. Sometimes the client's needs for help can be met by referral elsewhere. However, there are many occasions when there is no suitable help available in the public sector and clients simply cannot afford even low fees. Sinason (1997) suggests that in such cases the practitioner should share her professional and moral difficulties about this with the client rather than pretend enough has been given when the work is clearly incomplete. Not all practitoners would share this view as some would see taking the brunt of the client's anger as more therapeutic.

Another possible problem in the absence of clear organisational policy or guidelines about length of contracts is a kind of aimless drifting. Counsellors may fall into offering most clients long-term or at least open-ended contracts without first assessing and discussing their needs and wishes. Some clients may go along with this undefined situation but feel rather puzzled about what is supposed to be happening; others will vanish leaving the counsellor feeling inadequate. It is always important to ask oneself and the client what the client thinks he or she is coming for and to reach a shared and explicit understanding, although, as was the case with Pamela, the process of negotiation may not happen initially as it has to await the client's readiness to engage in it.

If potential long-term clients are currently receiving medical or psychiatric help counsellors may need to obtain their permission to discuss the proposed counselling with the doctor concerned. Similarly, liaison with other professionals is necessary should clients become involved with the psychiatric services while engaged in counselling. Our case study of David provides a good example of constructive joint working with medical services.

Membership of a professional body will provide counsellors with the resource of agreed policy, information and support about common issues and clients with the protection of a code of ethics and access to a complaints procedure. Counsellors need to arrange or check that their employers have arranged suitable professional indemnity insurance.

Resource network
Individual counselling, particularly with long-term clients, involves immersion in others' internal worlds and in a very special kind of relationship. To provide a perspective on this intensity, counsellors

need a professional culture in which to embed themselves and
ongoing support from colleagues as well as from a supervisor.
They need to be able to consult their peers, know whom they
might refer to and compare their experiences and learning. There
is a place for both everyday informal exchanges and the formalised
regular support of reading groups, workshops and short courses.
This is particularly important for counsellors working in isolation
either in an institution or privately. Such support structures are an
important part of ongoing professional development.

Time spent on establishing good working relationships with
professionals in other caring roles within one's own organisation or
in the wider community builds up a useful network of resources
for expert opinion, referral and emergency backup. Again David,
the ex-psychiatric patient described in Chapter 3, illustrates how
crucial these can be.

However, it is possible to get too involved in the counselling
world to the exclusion of other interests, activities or ways of
viewing the world. Too much of a good thing can make for an
unbalanced outlook and tired, tedious, inappropriately proselytis-
ing or unimaginative counsellors.

Personal suitability. Is there a fit between my strengths and the qualities necessary for this kind of work?

Much has been written on the personal qualities necessary for
becoming a counsellor. Although there are differences of emphasis
between orientations, most practitioners would agree that
counselling calls for basic trustworthiness, a capacity for empathy,
a willingness to be open to a range of feelings and an ability to
make, sustain and enjoy relationships while remaining conscious
of professional and ethical responsibilities. Counsellors need a
genuine concern for and curiosity about others, together with a
clear recognition of the other's 'equivalent centre of self, whence
the lights and shadows must always fall with a certain difference'
(Eliot, 1965: 243) in order to put the other first for the duration of
the session. They need a capacity to think about the process,
including how they might be being seen by different clients.

Do practitioners of long-term work need any particular qualities?
As long-term work will be likely to stir up strong, negative and
ambivalent feelings in the client, counsellors will need to be

personally robust to withstand and process what Elton Wilson describes as 'hidden areas of shame, rage, desire and dependency, as they erupt into the therapeutic relationship' (1996: 135). Patience, the capacity to stay calmly with regressed or erotically attached clients if necessary and the ability to defer gratification and to trust oneself and the process through difficult and stuck patches of the work all help. We would also suggest that long-term work is likely to call for the capacity to address how the counsellor is being perceived and used in the relationship, what psychodynamic counsellors see as the transference. Of course all of these qualities are useful in short-term work; we are writing here about differences of emphasis, not of kind.

Is this a time when I might realistically make a long-term commitment to a client?

This question is partly about practicalities and partly about emotional and mental space. Offering a client a long-term, open-ended commitment implies that one is reasonably sure to be in the same place and able to work for the foreseeable future. Counsellors new to this work may underestimate how important they may become to their clients; it is essential that they assess their own situation before taking on the responsibility it entails. One needs to be confident too that contact outside sessions (often inevitable in small towns or limited professional circles) can be managed. If the counsellor is uncertain about any of this it might be preferable to refer to a colleague who is more settled or more separate or, should this not be possible, to offer a time-limited contract. Anyone's circumstances can change unexpectedly but counsellors should not start work knowing they cannot finish it. Hence, if it seems likely that they may soon change jobs or geographical location, become pregnant, retire or take a prolonged break from work or if they have reason to be uncertain about their continued good health, they should not offer long-term work as this carries an implicit promise of reliability and stability. These are necessary elements if clients are to be free to explore their vulnerabilities and conflicts. It is not ethical to encourage someone to do this unless one is able to stay with them through the process. Indeed Daines et al. argue:

> Someone considering training for long-term, particularly psychodynamic, counselling and who generally has several weeks a year off ill

or receiving medical treatment, either because of an ongoing chronic illness, or susceptibility to whatever viruses are going round, should seriously consider whether it is the right occupation to enter. This may seem harsh, but many, if not most, clients have suffered from inconsistent or absent parents and it is unhelpful if this is reinforced by the counsellor's absences. (Daines et al., 1997: 26)

Similar considerations apply to other situations which might disrupt long-term counselling. For example, May's counsellor acknowledged the commitment he had made to her and therefore opted to carry on the work despite his wish to devote his energies to training and supervision and to further his professional development in that way.

Any new client seeking long-term work needs to be thought about in the context of the counsellor's overall caseload. Counsellors need more than the hour a week it takes to see a new client – they need time to reflect on and process their experience with different people. We would therefore warn against squeezing someone into an already overstretched schedule. Even if the time is available many counsellors feel the need to have a balance in the kind of issues or personality structures they are dealing with. Here individual strengths and inclinations come into play but most practitioners would feel burdened by and do well to avoid having many (or some would say any) suicidal, borderline or severely depressed clients at any one time. One of the authors recalls the strain of a year managing a service, personal difficulties and a caseload where several of her clients had attempted or ruminated about suicide. Syme points out:

> This work might involve considerable regression and dependency, which demands much more support and time than is usual. There may be times when a client becomes so regressed that they need more sessions a week than have been agreed at the outset. (Syme, 1994: 45)

She is referring to the extra demands which some more troubled long-term clients may make when they are relinquishing unhelpful coping strategies and have not yet found ways of holding themselves. Counsellors need to leave themselves some leeway in time and energy to respond in these circumstances.

Counsellors need to think about their own emotional state before committing themselves to clients, about whether they have the resilience necessary for this kind of engagement at this point in time. Like everyone else counsellors are subject to internal and

external upheavals. Counselling can be stressful work and practitioners need to be aware of and confident about maintaining their
own levels of receptivity and helpful curiosity as these are so
necessary for sustaining the involvement with someone in distress.

Some counsellors will want to focus on long-term work while
others will prefer a mixture of lengths of contract. As Coren (1996)
has pointed out, a succession of short-term clients is no easy
option, calling as this does for the ability to be adaptable, quick
thinking, clear about grasping central issues and finding acceptable
ways to convey these to the client. Long-term clients may provide
the opportunity to work at a more leisurely pace, following the
material as it arises. Combining the kinds of work may allow the
counsellor to use a range of skills and to apply the learning from
one way of working to the other.

Why do I want to do this kind of counselling?

We would suggest that it is helpful for counsellors to be clear about
their conscious and unconscious motives for undertaking this work
and realistic about the rewards and pitfalls they may encounter. We
are advocating self-knowledge rather than an impossible purity as
all of us do this work for a variety of reasons. It has become a truism
that many people are drawn to counselling as to the other caring
professions partly by a wish to care for their own needs projected
into others. Kleinians would argue that one reason for doing this
kind of work is unconscious guilt and the attempt to make
reparation for real or imagined attacks on internalised representa-
tions of important figures from past and present. These issues can
of course be explored in counsellors' personal therapy.

Storr offers a humane discussion of the reasons for this career
choice (1979: 164–85). He gives a very balanced view of the
double-edged gifts, histories and personality traits which may equip
people for therapeutic work and advocates a good enough level of
stability rather than an impossibly perfect standard of mental health.

> Mental health is not to be defined as the absence of problems. The
> only persons who have no problems are those that are dead, or else so
> rigid and unaware of themselves that they have ceased to develop.
> (Storr, 1979: 180)

On a more conscious level counsellors may be prepared and
eager to embark on long-term counselling for all kinds of reasons.

Most obviously, and most importantly, they realise that there is necessary and useful work to do. They may also have legitimate personal reasons such as being in training, just beginning in practice, keen to prove themselves in a new job or to a group of colleagues and therefore especially keen to develop and display the necessary skills and sensitivity. If in private practice they may need the financial security of knowing they have regular clients. They may have gained a great deal from their own therapy and be eager to share their rich experience with others.

However, counsellors may need to consider with each prospective client whether they are imposing their own needs or responding to what the client needs, wants and can manage. It is fine to want the best for a client, for him or her to have the opportunity to explore all possible issues, but the wish has to be a shared one and the realistic conditions for fulfilling it in place for the work to be successful. In our experience people new to counselling are sometimes over-enthusiastic about what it can achieve. They find it hard to let the client go before all issues seem to be resolved and thus can burden clients with an unwanted therapeutic perfectionism and themselves with an unnecessary sense of failure when initial contacts do not develop into long-term work. The counsellor we have described working with Tom provides an example of this tendency.

All good counselling makes particular demands on the practitioner's skills and self and carries some satisfaction. We all need some rewards from our work, but not of course at our clients' expense. It may be permissible to enjoy feeling needed or helpful – these are ordinary enough human responses but they do require scrutiny. Pamela, one of our case examples, enjoyed feeling her daughter's reliance on her but in fostering it she was undermining her daughter's legitimate strivings for independence and autonomy. Counsellors too may fall into this trap. Those who require – consciously or more usually unconsciously – clients to reassure them about their own worth may be dodging valid criticism or depriving clients of the valuable opportunity to explore negative feelings with someone who will be neither overwhelmed nor retaliatory. They may hang on to a client unnecessarily so that they, like Pamela, can feel needed.

Counsellors may seem to share problematic areas with their clients. The impetus to understand these may be helpful for both but there is a danger of counsellors holding on to such clients as a way of working on personal issues secondhand or of misperceiving the clients' issues because of their own.

There can be an intensity to a therapeutic relationship which is not often encountered in daily life. Sometimes this can arouse a certain amount of envy in other workers in a team or even in a partner who may feel shut out. The potential intensity is undoubtedly one of the attractions of the work, but it should not become a substitute for intimacy in one's own private life. Sometimes clients are people whom one might hope to have as friends if met in another context. It can be very difficult to stay in role and act appropriately but authentically with such clients when one has an impulse to be self-revelatory or to suggest a different kind of relationship after counselling has ended. Occasionally too, as with our imaginary client May, counsellors and clients may be sexually attracted to each other, an attraction made more likely by the intimacy of the counselling situation. In our view there are no exceptions to the rule forbidding sexual contact between counsellor and client, however beguiling the prospect may appear. Bramley (1996a: 186–90) gives a salutary example of a reciprocated, although unenacted, erotic transference where unresolved issues for counsellor and client fitted in such a way as to foster a strong mutual attraction which needed supervisory work to protect the client's therapy and the counsellor's career.

One pleasure of long-term work is the sense of timelessness and relief from the feelings of urgency and crisis that can accompany shorter term work. Molnos (1995) writes vividly of the lure of timelessness and the danger of perfectionist tendencies. For some clients the sense of limitless time can be an invitation to defer change. Knowing whom they are going to see at the same time every week provides long-term counsellors with the security of a predictable structure. There is a danger that without the pressure of a time limit counsellor and client may get fixed into a cosy but repetitive pattern. Counsellors may simply run out of steam and find nothing new to say and yet find it hard to terminate if they are dependent in their own way on clients they have come to know well and enjoy.

That said, for some clients long-term work is necessary and it can be immensely rewarding for both counsellor and client. A long-term relationship that is alive is necessarily a shifting and complex one. Of course the counsellor is there to be used by the client. Nonetheless it is fascinating for counsellors to have different parts of themselves evoked and to have the time to get to know clients in depth. One of our respondents wrote of the pleasure of long-term work:

> The pleasure of seeing the client grow and change, move through dependence and attachment to independence; developing a deeper relationship with the client, which is also one of the main sources of difficulty as well as pleasure. The relationship with a long-term client becomes much more complex than with a short-term client as there is time for such development.

Many clients are not going to be able to share or even be in private touch with painful experiences and feelings without the safety of long-term support. This would account for one of our clients who never had an actual memory of being sexually abused as a very young child but who dreamt about the experience very clearly some four years into counselling at a time when she perceived her own daughter to be at risk. During the course of long-term work clients inevitably have a variety of life experiences which may bring different parts of a personality and past into focus. For example, many students find the prospect of graduation can crystallise conflicts about accepting adult status and finally separating from parental protection. Illness or the death of someone close may lead to periods of intense self-questioning.

What does this particular client evoke in me?

We have discussed motives for undertaking this work in general but each new potential client may pose particular questions for the counsellor. However much work we may have done on ourselves, we all have blind spots or perhaps issues which are particularly sensitive and current in our own lives. Counsellors who know they are still very confused or raw about an area might consider referring people whom they recognise need to deal with similar issues. Cruse, the national agency which offers counselling to people who have been bereaved, recognises the dangers of confusing personal and client issues by not accepting for training anyone who has been bereaved in the two years prior to application.

This personal response needs to be distinguished from another kind of countertransference response which can be more useful to the client because it provides information about what unwanted or frightening parts of the self the client may be projecting into the counsellor or the kind of relationship the client is trying to set up. For example, Pamela made her counsellor feel quite powerless at the initial interview. Instead of acting on this by refusing any help the counsellor used her capacity to analyse her own feelings to understand just how helpless Pamela might be feeling.

What if the counsellor gets ill?

Daines et al. (1997) discuss this possibility. They point out that the counsellor needs to consider how much information to give the client and the extent to which this might inhibit the range of client's responses. The sudden hospitalisation of Joy's counsellor prompted a very important development in their relationship in that it helped Joy to experience and express some of her more negative feelings. The same authors draw attention to the possibility that 'some medical or psychiatric conditions should lead counsellors to consider stopping their practice' (1997: 29), and to the responsibility of colleagues and supervisors to intervene if they consider a counsellor's physical or psychological condition to be undermining professional competence.

What if things go wrong?

This question was addressed more fully in the last chapter. Some counsellors advocate structuring regular review sessions with the client even with long-term, open-ended work. They would see these as a way of countering the dangers of drifting on in a rather aimless fashion, becoming cosily collusive with a client's difficulties or of both parties just being insufficiently unaware of the other's thoughts about and experience of the process. Other counsellors might feel that formal reviewing interrupted the development of a transference relationship. Whatever decision is made, counsellors need to be constantly reviewing their work and the state of the relationship with the client. They might consider whether clients are becoming so dependent on weekly support that they are unlikely ever to be able to manage without it, potentially a very dangerous situation. Counsellors will review both on their own and with their supervisors. No one can predict all difficulties at assessment or avoid them in the course of the work but counsellors can be honest about their uncertainties and mistakes and willing to let a more experienced clinician look at their practice and offer a fresh, although sometimes disconcerting, perspective.

This is particularly important when things seem to be going badly wrong. Possibly the worst scenario would be finding oneself with a regressed, vulnerable client who wanted to keep on working even though the counsellor feels out of his or her depth. The counsellor may not be able to find a suitable colleague to take a referral or the client may refuse to accept one. It may be difficult to accept that there are circumstances where the best option is no counselling at all. It is not possible to provide a general prescription that will suit every case but we would re-emphasise the importance of therapy for awareness of oneself, of supervision for awareness of the dynamic between client and counsellor and a professional support network for familiarity with medical and psychiatric facilities which are available for all, even when ongoing psychological therapy is not.

Ongoing development

Paradoxically, difficulties may turn out to be helpful in that they can alert counsellors to the need for further professional development and direct attention to the issues they need to address. Learning in this field should be an ongoing activity. Counsellors, we hope, continue to reflect on their own life experiences and those – good and bad – with clients. This reflection may lead to a wish to re-enter therapy, find a more challenging kind of supervision or undertake further training. Such steps are not indications of failure but signs of healthy regard for oneself and one's clients.

7

Final Thoughts

In this book we have tried to indicate the potential advantages of long-term counselling for clients and some of the pleasures and difficulties that counsellors may encounter in the process of working with them. Throughout we have been concerned to emphasise the importance of professional and ethical practice. In this final chapter we will explore how research and evaluation might support good practice and discuss how counsellors might make the case for the provision of long-term counselling in their employing institutions. We will also return briefly to the issue of professional development for this work.

The apparently leisurely pace and discursiveness of long-term counselling goes against the grain of much in contemporary society with its emphasis on activity, speed and immediately measurable gains. This means that practitioners will often be called upon by managers and sometimes by potential clients and colleagues who use different methods to justify their choice of this method of working. Responses would of course vary, depending on an understanding of what might lie behind the question, but should be informed by a knowledge of the issues explored in the current literature on research and evaluation as well as on personal conviction.

Self-monitoring

Whether or not counsellors are accountable to an institution, they benefit from questioning and reflecting on their own practice and from clarity about the philosophy and values implicit in it. Clients invest considerable hope, time, energy and sometimes money in long-term counselling; they are entitled to expect such reflection and clarity from their counsellors.

Every counselling contract needs to be evaluated. We would suggest that just as assessment does not happen only at the beginning of a piece of long-term work, so evaluation should not happen only at the end. All counselling work should be subject to ongoing evaluation by the counsellor's own private appraisal, discussion in supervision and sensitivity to clients' reactions, whether or not these are elicited in formal review sessions. An ending often provides the stimulus for further reflection on the work, whether as an attempt to understand the reason for an abrupt breaking off by the client or in preparation for a planned termination of a contract. Over time individual counsellors need to build up a picture of their competence with different types of person and difficulties and learn to make a judgement about those whom they might do well to refer elsewhere unless or until they have undertaken further training.

Evaluation, research and counsellor attitudes

However, we would suggest that there is a need for more formal kinds of assessment as well as that provided by the counsellor's private self-scrutiny. Barker et al. (1994) describe evaluation as 'applied research into the implementation and effectiveness of clinical services designed to answer two central questions – "What are you trying to do?" and "How will you know if you've done it?"' (1994: 197). A BAC publication argues:

> Proper evaluation of counselling is both ethical and desirable as a response to demands from funders for evidence of 'value for money' and as a way to increase counsellors' self-knowledge. Evaluation means the clarification of aims and definitions of measures of attainment as well as the systematic collection and consideration of information to inform decisions about efficiency, resource allocation and effectiveness. It is an essential and enabling aspect of practice which can benefit clients, counsellors, employing agencies and funders. (BAC Information Sheet no. 13)

Despite this exhortation and a growing literature on methods for evaluating counselling and psychotherapy, counsellors are often somewhat resistant to using or undertaking formal evaluation or research studies (Shipton, 1996). Any method of research carries a risk of contaminating the therapeutic relationship and many counsellors object to research principally on these clinical grounds, particularly where the long-term evolution of the therapeutic relationship is paramount. Many fear that research and evaluation activities may interfere with the privacy of the two-person counselling relationship or fail to account adequately for its subtlety. Many think it intrusive to follow up clients after the work is completed and feel distaste for some common methods of evaluating counselling work such as the use of video and audio tapes, asking clients to complete standardised before and after psychological tests or seeking feedback through questionnaires/interviews.

There are of course ethical and transference issues as well as practical difficulties involved in assessing counsellors' work by the use of psychological tests, questionnaires and follow-up interviews but there is some evidence to suggest that the resistance to evaluation and research lies more with counsellors than clients who are often reported to be pleased to be asked their opinion and to see research activity as proof that a service or agency takes its work seriously. Counsellors working in an agency setting have the opportunity to engage in evaluation and research with their colleagues but may fear having their work exposed and compared to that of others and so obstruct the process.

It may be that the increased emphasis on research in professional counselling training courses and the growth of counselling psychology as a profession can produce counsellors who have specialised training in research methodologies (see *Counselling Psychology Review*, 1996, for many useful papers on approaches to researching counselling). People who wish to argue for the retention of long-term approaches to helping in the NHS and other agencies of provision feel there is an urgent need to furnish good evidence to support their case, as argued by Parry (1996). Others may be interested in research of a 'purer' kind. All counsellors are faced with the double bind of counselling having achieved much more recognition and some idealisation in the press and media while also being repeatedly attacked and denigrated. To protect both client provision and their own livelihood, the professions involved in long-term counselling need evaluation and research.

There has been an upsurge of interest in research in recent years; indeed the authors met when they were members of the Research Sub-Committee of the Association for Student Counselling. Both would argue that there is much to be gained from persisting with research and evaluation projects, despite the difficulties that might be encountered.

Some approaches to evaluation worth consulting

The BAC has produced a number of publications which may prove helpful. These include the information sheet on evaluation and counselling quoted above, a set of ethical guidelines for monitoring, evaluating and research in counselling and a number of selected references about the effectiveness of counselling in a range of settings (medicine, bereavement, higher education, primary care, the workplace, eating disorders, sexual abuse). Also available from BAC is *A Guide to Recognising Best Practice in Counselling* which raises questions about both the individual counsellor's capacity to think about his or her work and about institutional provision. The current authors have edited a series of conference papers entitled *Perspectives on Evaluation and Research in Counselling* (1993). This publication explores the dynamics of evaluation, describes two contrasting methods of assessing the effectiveness of counselling and summarises the workshops and debates of the conference.

Recent influential work in this area includes Shapiro and Barkham's (1993) study for Relate, the Leeds Psychological Therapies Research Centre evaluation project, and Roth and Fonagy's (1996) study *What Works for Whom?* on therapeutic provision in the NHS which was commissioned by the Department of Health. The report on the Relate evaluative research describes the benefits of completed counselling as including considerable reduction in the severity of mental health problems and improvement in relations between partners and comments interestingly on the process of introducing a research culture into an organisation. (For further commentary see Mellor-Clark and Shapiro, 1995.) The counselling evaluated there was largely short-term; it formed one part of Relate's strategy to establish research as a continuing part of the organisation's work.

Researchers at the Psychological Therapies Research Centre at the University of Leeds reported on their current work at the 1997 BAC Research Conference. They have devised 34 core questions which are seen as a definitive synthesis of previous test questions.

They cover the four areas of subjective well-being, symptoms, life/ social functioning, and risk/harm to self and others. They suggest asking these questions before and after counselling as well as monthly during the contract. Their proposal is that counselling agencies should buy into this scheme and send their completed questionnaires to Leeds for scoring; the project may gain widespread support. We suspect this approach may prove more suitable for gauging the effectiveness of brief counselling interventions and leave long-term counsellors looking for additional measures.

Roth and Fonagy's conclusions are also rather disappointing for advocates of long-term help. They draw largely on empirical research and randomised control trials. They conclude that the case for long-term therapeutic interventions is not proven. They point to the comparative lack of research studies in psychodynamic therapy which they explain by 'the absence of a quantative research tradition within this orientation – the expense and difficulty of mounting trials of long-term treatment and the absence of appropriate measures to encompass the more ambitious aims of these treatments' (1996: 32). However, the 1995 joint report by the Royal College of Psychiatrists and British Psychological Society does argue that:

> Within the NHS priority should be given to people with more severe psychological problems for whom treatment might have to be long-term in order to be effective. It is as cost-inefficient to provide short-term therapies which are not effective as it is to provide long-term therapies where short-term therapies would be as effective. (1995: 10)

Oldfield (1983) studied clients' experiences of counselling – including some long-term – at the Isis Centre in Oxford. Although written some time ago, her book is still well worth reading for its thoughtful discussion of a respectful and thorough approach to evaluation without intruding on or pressurising clients.

Penny Spearman of WPF Counselling, probably the largest provider of long-term counselling in the UK, has been seconded by that organisation to study methods of evaluating counselling. Her aim is to define effectiveness and safety in counselling; she means, like Oldfield, to prioritise the client's viewpoint and is developing ethical and reliable methods of gathering evidence from former users of counselling.

What agencies might do

Counselling agencies may wish to evaluate service delivery – for example, clients' and referrers' perceptions of accessibility, waiting times, reception arrangements, confidence in confidentiality. Such areas are generally experienced by counsellors as less contentious than evaluating the success of counselling itself, particularly when this is done through heavy reliance on client perception. However, agencies can attempt to evaluate outcome and are able to use less personalised follow-up methods than private counsellors as it is possible to arrange for another counsellor or outside evaluator to interview former clients or analyse their questionnaires if these are the chosen research tools.

We would suggest that some agencies might well undertake some broader evaluation: they can keep a record of what happens to clients who have been offered long-term work; try to understand why some drop out and others complete. This might help to inform future practice about assessment and allocation. An agency which offers short- as well as long-term counselling might be able to do some comparative study. Of particular interest might be clients returning for further help after an initial brief intervention. Not every service can evaluate everything but there is scope for co-operation between agencies on evaluative projects and for learning from experience elsewhere in the field.

Methodological issues in research into long-term counselling

There is an overlap between evaluation and research, which tends to be more concerned with the discovery of new knowledge, to be more interested in theory, to take place in a controlled academic environment and to be generalisible. For those unsure about or unfamiliar with an evaluation and research approach we recommend Mcleod (1994) and Barker et al. (1994).

Most research in counselling and psychotherapy is based on short-term approaches which are more amenable to the observable measurement of change; this means that there is a paucity of data about the kinds of long-term work described in this book. Any perusal of research studies will also reveal that counsellors and psychotherapists are often lumped together for the benefit of researchers. A bigger divide has existed historically between researchers and practitioners in both counselling and psychotherapy (Watkins and Schneider, 1991; Shipton, 1994) than between counsellors and psychotherapists.

Research is often shaped by drug trial methodology and the simplification of therapeutic processes required by quantitative approaches. This echoes the identification in Chapter 2 of the medical model as a powerful influence. However, qualitative approaches have become increasingly attractive to researchers, especially with the development of discourse analysis and related disciplines, but they are conceptually very difficult and need time to be learned. It seems that counsellors who wish to evaluate their work or carry out original research need more than training; they also need support, both economically and intellectually.

What can we learn from the research on long-term work?

Despite all the difficulties over methodology there is a legacy of research which counsellors can claim, though little refers explicitly to long-term counselling. Barkham (1996) has identified four generations of research in psychotherapy which may help counsellors to orientate themselves in this now extensive field. The first generation started with Eysenck's (1952) critique of psychotherapy and focused on outcome research to assess just how effective or ineffective psychotherapeutic treatment was in comparison to no treatment or placebo treatment. It became clear that, contrary to Eysenck's conclusion, psychotherapy was significantly more helpful to clients than no intervention and that placebos were not neutral and could not be administered in a vacuum where the supplier's personal qualities did not play a part.

A need to target specific factors led to a second generation of enquiry when researchers sought evidence to support or argue against the myth of uniformity whereby differences between clients, therapists, therapies and lengths of treatment time had been neglected. In this 'wave' clients would often be allocated to random control groups and differences in outcome were scrutinised, with a view to determining which clients did well with which approaches. Greater specificity about the process of therapy led to inconclusive discussions about the role of the facilitative conditions in successful outcome. The single case study – the crucial clinical and training tool used in counselling – came back into favour as a respectable approach to studying counselling and psychotherapy. A fourth generation has emphasised cost effectiveness and service delivery. This wave of research has often been deeply unimpressed by long-term help, although researchers have produced some findings which are relevant to the arguments in this book and to which we will return. Readers are recommended to Barkham's (1996) erudite and lucid chapter, though it is geared to 'individual therapy' rather than long-term counselling.

Denman (1995: 175) provides on overview of research specifically about long-term therapy which she defines as 'therapy lasting upwards of two years at intensities varying from once a week to five times a week'. While this excludes some of our cases, it remains very useful for others. Furthermore, Denman identifies three areas of research which need to be done. First, there is the need for providers of services to be able to ascertain which clients or patients get which treatment and which people should be denied long-term approaches with a clear, agreed definition of long-term. This is in keeping with Barkham's fourth generation classification. Although it directly concerns only counsellors who are employed by large service providers, it probably affects the public perception of all long-term counselling.

The second area is clinical and involves a host of research questions. When should extra sessions be given, for example? How should regression best be managed (an important issue for counsellors who, in the schema outlined in Chapter 2, would be avoiding active work with regression)? How should termination be handled? Such issues and others are of relevance to counsellors and psychotherapists wherever they work.

The third area is inquiry into the very process of counselling and psychotherapy. What brings about change and how is it evidenced? What can we can tell from the long-term intimate relations we establish in our professional work about how the mind seems to work? This level of research is perhaps the most challenging and the most underfunded but is the one that is most congruent with the reflective processes of counsellors who, week-in, week-out, observe minute shifts and turns in their relationships with long-term clients as well as the more global changes for better or worse. However, it is perhaps only the most exceptional people who have advanced theory and practice in this domain. Although many counsellors would not wish to enter into debates about the mind, it is in long-term approaches that a great opportunity exists to produce clinically useful research.

Advocates of short-term counselling (see Feltham, 1997) often refer to research which shows that clients improve after only a few sessions. However, time is an ally as well as a suspicious thief if we take seriously some of the more recent research. Howard et al. (1986), in an analysis of 110 out of 114 estimates of the relation between amount of treatment and outcome, found a positive link between number of sessions and successful outcome in psychotherapy. Using the old drug dosage analogy mentioned previously, but with a great deal of thoughtfulness and mathematical acumen, the researchers applied proper drug dosage criteria to their analysis. They used a quantity of psychotherapy like a weight of drugs and, as in drug trials, took the criterion of effective exposure to treatment in pharmacological studies as the dosage at which 50 per cent of patients showed some response. They suggest:

> If this criterion were adopted for psychotherapy research, the present results indicate that the dosage for establishing a treatment group would generally be six to eight sessions (this could be modified to fit the particular diagnostic categories and outcome criteria included in a specific study). Subjects (patients) who have had less than six to eight sessions should be considered, for purposes of research, as not having been effectively exposed to treatment and should be analysed separately (as should dropouts, refusers, etc.). (Howard et al., 1986: 163)

Howard's meta-analysis indicates that by 26 sessions, three-quarters of the patients had improved. We should be wary of becoming too seduced by the power of such mathematical arguments in cost-cutting times, especially if clinical judgement is initially unnecessarily pessimistic, as was shown in one study (Benedek, 1992). However, Howard and his colleagues draw quite heartening conclusions:

> No treatment is 100% effective in alleviating any disorder. It seems safe to assume that a single course of psychotherapy [not defined in the paper] would result in measurable improvement for at most about 85% of the patients that enter this form of treatment. From our analysis, it would appear that for the average patient sample, the maximum percentage improved would be reached in approximately 52 once-weekly sessions. Of course . . . some patients may feel or show improvement in fewer

sessions, and others may require more treatment. Further analysis of patient characteristics and specific outcome criteria will certainly be required before firm and fair standards can be set. (Howard et al., 1986: 164)

The notion of a 'firm' standard is rather intimidating and the statistical complexity of 'probit analysis' used in Howard's research is daunting. Although it is difficult to prove, methodologies which are very far removed from clinical methods would not, to our minds, be sensitive to the kind of clinical issues professional counsellors wish to illuminate. It is up to counsellors themselves to take up the challenge, perhaps in collaboration with research scientists and social scientists because, as it stands at the moment, there is no hard evidence that long-term counselling is better than short-term. We do know that Seligman (1996) found that a significant proportion of 'consumers' were happier with it than with short-term approaches and that Chiesa et al. (1996) have demonstrated that it is cost effective for some people to receive long-term help.

The longer the counselling, the harder it is to be specific about change factors since life circumstances change people and make their influence felt and underlying issues emerge and are worked through or go underground with a rhythm that is unique to each counselling relationship. The role of life circumstances has been given some thought by Parkes (1980) who reviewed the research literature on the effects of bereavement counselling. He found it was likely to help prevent the formation of clinical syndromes in the bereaved. The role of bereavement counselling in the alleviation of distress and prevention of illness, whether physical or psychological, is a good example of the difficulty in thinking about counselling and research. Time would have helped heal the pain that May was trying to stave off as she had to face up to her losses and their intensification at key times of the year such as Christmas and anniversaries, but we cannot know how she would have managed without assistance or how it would have been if the counsellor had decided to offer only brief or intermittent help. Similarly, other individuals mentioned in this book negotiated, like we all do, changes and pressures in everyday life which were not necessarily present at the beginning of their counselling. In this respect, long-term counsellors' capacity to bend with the flow of the client's material is not a sign of inadequacy and loss of direction, but sensitive attunement to a changing other with whom a relationship develops.

Making the case for long-term counselling in institutions

Given recent changes in the structure and culture of our public institutions it is far from easy to convince managers and funders of the value of providing long-term counselling. Health, welfare and educational organisations all have many calls on restricted budgets; competition for voluntary sector funding is also fierce. There have been attempts, many successful, to close institutions specialising in the provision of intensive psychotherapeutic support. Holmes (1992), Sinason (1997) and Wilson (1997) all make powerful cases for long-term work in the public sector but it has to be acknowledged that in the last resort they are arguing from a set of beliefs and values which may not be convincing to many budget holders, given the hold market values have taken on the discourse about public services and welfare. Dependency is often depicted as undesirable and quick results are often sought. Counselling cannot avoid dealing with the former or promise the latter. Moreover the profession itself frequently gets a bad press. See Smith (1997) for a discussion of the difficulties of representing counselling values in institutions dominated by survival anxieties and the possible consequences for counsellors' morale, integrity and sense of identity.

We believe it would be regrettable if long-term counselling were to flourish only in private practice, thus restricting access for those on low incomes. We should like to see the widespread provision of free and low-cost counselling – of the length the client needs – in a range of public and voluntary settings so that it can be available to all who may benefit. The gap between the ways of thinking and approaches to evaluation familiar to purchasers and providers of counselling is very marked. We would suggest that there is a need to continue the argument, however dispiriting constant justification of the value of what we offer can be and however daunting the challenge of trying to integrate views from two opposite starting points. The approach adopted by Relate of trying to build up a research base that will both inform counselling practice and provide support for funding bids makes strategic sense.

Those responsible for making a case for funding for this work may need to begin by trying to understand the concerns and anxieties of budget holders and learning to speak their language. Hence it might be useful in a health service setting to point out that the provision of counselling may save expenditure on drugs, GP consultations and possibly hospitalisation. In a university setting the case may be made that intensive help for particularly distressed clients could reduce the likelihood of disturbance and disruption in teaching and residential groups, save the time and energy of academic and administrative staff, reduce student discontinuation rates and the possibility of adverse publicity should students act out their distress by suicide or other violent activity. Denman (1994) and Healy (1994) make the case for justifying their psychotherapy services in the cost-benefit terms of the market while Tolley and Rowland (1995) consider ways of evaluating the cost effectiveness of counselling in healthcare settings.

We have a great deal of respect for those who have sought to develop group work and brief effective forms of counselling and psychotherapy so that help can be available to more people. We suggest it may be easier to make a case for some long-term provision when a unit has explored the potential of other approaches and is offering a range of counselling interventions to suit different needs. Knowledge of the research literature and clarity about the grounds for the recommendation of long-term counselling, its goals and the methods of evaluating the work are all necessary if a convincing argument is to be made.

Developing and monitoring professional competence

Throughout we have been arguing the importance of reflective practice and ongoing learning for this work. The BAC requires evidence of ongoing professional development when practitioners apply for re-accreditation. Such development might be achieved by a number of routes or combination of them.

Individuals might well look for further training in long-term work. At the moment this is difficult because of the considerable lack of parity between trainings and the resultant confusion (Potter, 1997); it cannot be assumed that any one degree or diploma is roughly equivalent to another. On the whole advanced specialist training in counselling, unlike in social work, is not available. The previous chapter suggested that initial training courses might perhaps pay more attention to the differences connected with the length of counselling and the qualities and skills relevant to working in different time scales. Some initial trainings do offer a master's degree which may be taken after a break for the consolidation of learning, and there are opportunities for higher research degrees but we know of relatively few courses which provide certification for experienced counsellors wishing to further their clinical development by formal study after some years of practice. We think there may be a place for an expansion in the provision of such advanced clinical courses. These would ask for a fair amount of post-qualification experience and would provide the opportunity to reflect on accumulated clinical experience in some depth, to look at one's practice afresh, to learn from one's peers, revisit and re-examine familiar concepts and study recent literature in the field. Training in supervision is becoming increasingly available; learning to become an accomplished supervisor is another way of developing clinical expertise.

Ongoing supervision of one's own counselling which we have already discussed in previous chapters is a vital tool for monitoring and continuing one's learning. On the same principle we would suggest that personal therapy is not necessarily a once and for all activity for counsellors. A return to therapy after a break may lead to fresh understandings and a revitalised way of working.

Wilkins (1997) stresses the interconnectedness of professional and personal development for counsellors and discusses other ways in which they might further their learning. These include study of different orientations from that of one's original training, keeping professional logs, teaching, running workshops, reading, writing and research activity. For those with access to the Internet we would add joining some of the relevant e-mail discussion forums such as the one on psychotherapy and counselling (psych-couns@mailbase.ac.uk) which provide the opportunity for the exchange of views on professional matters with colleagues throughout the world.

Conclusion

Ultimately our belief in the importance of the availability of long-term counselling is an expression of certain values. Having sufficient time to do something properly is not a luxury, although our present culture may represent it as such. The sense of timelessness may indeed be a lure but it can also be a relief from unremitting pressure to perform or to fill up time rather mindlessly with a huge number of tasted but half-digested experiences. In contrast we would emphasise the importance of what long-term counselling can offer: close, detailed attention to the complexity and richness of human experience; the centrality of a committed relationship; belief in the possibility of development. In arguing that most of us can always discover more about ourselves in long-term work, we are not advocating a search for impossible perfection or counselling without end but drawing attention to the pleasures of curiosity and self-discovery and the sustenance of hope which such counselling can provide.

References

APA (1994) *Diagnostic and Statistical Manual of Mental Disorders: DSM-IV^{TM}*. Washington, DC: American Psychiatric Association.

ASC (no date given) *A Guide to Recognising Best Practice in Counselling*. Rugby: Association for Student Counselling.

BAC (1993) *Membership Survey 1993*. Rugby: British Association for Counselling.

BAC Information Guide no. 4 (1996) *Ethical Guidelines for Monitoring, Research and Evaluation in Counselling*. Rugby: British Association for Counselling.

BAC Information Sheet no. 13 (undated) *Evaluation and Counselling*. Rugby: British Association for Counselling.

Barker, C., Pistrang, R. and Elliott, R. (1994) *Research Methods in Clinical and Counselling Psychology*. Chichester: John Wiley.

Barkham, M. (1989) Exploratory therapy in two-plus-one sessions, *British Journal of Psychotherapy*, 6 (1): 81–100.

Barkham, M. (1996) Individual therapy: process and outcome findings across successive research generations, in W. Dryden (ed.), *Handbook of Individual Therapy*. London: Sage. pp. 328–64.

Belkin, G. (1988) *Introduction to Counselling*. Dubuque, IA: Wm. C. Brown: 21–5.

Benedek, L. von (1992) The mental activity of the psychoanalyst, *Psychotherapy Research*, 2 (1): 63–72.

Bramley, W. (1996a) *The Broad Spectrum Psychotherapist*. London: Free Association Books.

Bramley, W. (1996b) *The Supervisory Couple in Broad Spectrum Psychotherapy*. London: Free Association Books.

Brennan, T. (1993) *History After Lacan*. London: Routledge.

Brown, D.G. (1977) Drowsiness in the countertransference, *International Journal of Psycho-Analysis*, 4: 481–92.

Brown, D. and Pedder, J. (1991) *Introduction to Psychotherapy*, 2nd edn. London: Routledge. First edition 1979.

Casement, P. (1990) *Further Learning From the Patient: The Analytic Space and Process*. London: Routledge.

Cawley, R.H. (1977) The teaching of psychotherapy, *Association of University Teachers of Psychiatry Newsletter*, January: 19–36.

Chiesa, M., Iacoponni, E. and Morris, M. (1996) Changes in health service utilization by patients with severe personality disorders before and after in-patient psychosocial treatment, *British Journal of Psychotherapy*, 12 (4): 501–12.

Coltart, N. (1987) Diagnosis and assessment for suitability for psycho-analytical psychotherapy, *British Journal of Psychotherapy*, 4 (2): 127–34.

Coren, A. (1996) Brief therapy – base metal or pure gold?, *Psychodynamic Counselling*, 2 (1): 22–38.

Counselling Psychology Review (1996) 11 (1).

Crisp, A.H. (1965) A treatment regime for anorexia nervosa, *British Journal of Psychiatry*, 112: 505–12.

Daines, B., Gask, L. and Usherwood, T. (1997) *Medical and Psychiatric Issues in Counselling*. London: Sage.

Denman, C. (1995) Questions to be answered in the evaluation of long-term therapy, in M. Aveline and D.A. Shapiro (eds), *Research Foundations for Psychotherapy Practice*. Chichester: John Wiley/Mental Health Foundation. pp. 175–90.

Denman, F. (1994) The value of psychotherapy, *British Journal of Psychotherapy*, 11 (2): 284–9.

Dryden, W. (1996) A rose by any other name: a personal view on the differences among professional titles, in I. James and S. Palmer (eds), *Professional Therapeutic Titles: Myths and Realities*. Leicester: British Psychological Society.

Dryden, W., Horton, I. and Mearns, D. (1995) *Issues in Professional Counsellor Training*. London: Cassell.

Dryden, W. and Thorne, B. (eds) (1991) *Training and Supervision for Counselling in Action*. London: Sage.

Einzig, H. (1989) *Counselling and Psychotherapy: Is It For Me?* Rugby: British Association for Counselling.

Eliot, G. (1965) *Middlemarch*. London: Penguin.

Eliot, T.S. (1959) *Four Quartets*. London: Faber and Faber.

Elton Wilson, J. (1996) *Time-Conscious Psychological Therapy*. London: Routledge.

Eysenck, H. (1952) The effects of psychotherapy: an evaluation, *Journal of Consulting Psychology*, 16: 319–24.

Feltham, C. (1995) *What is Counselling?: The Promise and Problem of the Talking Therapies*. London: Sage.

Feltham, C. (1997) *Time-Limited Counselling*. London: Sage.

Feltham, C. and Dryden, W. (1994) *Developing Counsellor Supervision*. London: Sage.

Fonagy, P. (1991) Thinking about thinking: some clinical and theoretical considerations in the treatment of a borderline personality, *International Journal of Psycho-Analysis*, 72: 639–56.

Freud, S. (1913) On beginning the treatment, *Standard Edition 12*. pp. 123–44.

Freud, S. and Breuer, J. (1895) *Studies on Hysteria*, vol. 1. Penguin Freud Library, Pelican Books (1974). Reprinted Harmondsworth: Penguin (1991).

Frick, W.B. (1971) *Humanistic Psychology: Interviews with Maslow, Murphy and Rogers*. Columbus, OH: Charles E. Merrill.

Glueck, P. (1960) Psychoanalysis: reflections and comments, in P. Hoch and J. Zurbin (eds), *Current Approaches to Psychoanalysis*. New York and London: Grune and Stanton. pp. 123–40.

Gray, A. (1994) *An Introduction to the Therapeutic Frame*. London: Routledge.

Greenblatt, M. (1978) The grieving spouse, *American Journal of Psychiatry*, 135: 43–7.

Hall, Z., Mullee, M. and Thompson, C. (1995) A clinical and service evaluation of group therapy for women survivors of childhood sexual abuse, in A. Aveline and D.A. Shapiro (eds), *Research Foundations for Psychotherapy Practice*. Chichester: John Wiley.

Healy, K. (1994) Why purchase psychotherapy services?, *British Journal of Psychotherapy*, 11 (2): 279–83.

Henry, W.P. and Strupp, H.H. (1994) The therapeutic alliance as interpersonal process, in A.O. Horvath and L.S. Greenberg (eds), *The Working Alliance: Theory, Research and Practice*. New York: John Wiley.

Herman, J. and Schatzow, E. (1984) Time-limited group therapy for women with a history of incest, *International Journal of Group Psychotherapy*, 34 (4): 605–16.

Hermansson, G. (1996) E-mail discussion, Psych-Couns.

Holmes, J. (1992) Psychiatry without walls, *Psychoanalytic Psychotherapy*, 6 (1): 1–12.

Holmes, J. (1993) *Between Art and Science. Essays in Psychotherapy and Psychiatry*. London: Tavistock.

Holmes, J. (1995) How I assess for psychoanalytic psychotherapy, in C. Mace (ed.), *The Art and Science of Assessment in Psychotherapy*. London: Routledge.

Howard, K.I., Kopta, S.M., Krause, M.S. and Orlinsky, D.E. (1986) The dose-effect relationship in psychotherapy, *American Psychologist*, 41 (2): 159–64.

Hsu, G.L.K. (1990) *Eating Disorders*. New York: Guilford.

Jacobs, M. (1988) *Psychodynamic Counselling in Action*. London: Sage.

Jacobs, M. (1994) Psychodynamic counselling: an identity achieved?, *Psychodynamic Counselling*, 1 (1): 79–92.

Jacobs, M. (1996) *In Search of Supervision*. Buckingham: Open University Press.

James, I. and Palmer, S. (eds) (1996) *Professional Therapeutic Titles: Myths and Realities*. Leicester: British Psychological Society.

Kagan, N. (1980) *Interpersonal Process Recall: A Method of Influencing Human Interaction*. Houston, TX: Mason Media.

Kahn, M. (1991) *Between Therapist and Client: The New Relationship*. New York: Freeman.

Kelly, T.A. and Strupp, H.H. (1992) Patient and therapist values in psychotherapy: perceived changes, assimilation similarity, and outcome, *Journal of Consulting and Clinical Psychology*, 60 (1): 34–40.

Kirschenbaum, H. and Henderson, V.L. (eds) (1990) *The Carl Rogers Reader*. London: Constable.

Klein, J. (1995) *Doubts and Certainties in Psychotherapy*. London: Karnac.

Kübler-Ross, E. (1981) *Living with Death and Dying*. London: Souvenir Press.

Langs, R. (1994) *Doing Supervision and Being Supervised*. London: Karnac.

Lawrence, M. (1984) *The Anorexic Experience*. London: Women's Press.

Lazarus, A.A. (1989) *The Practice of Multimodal Therapy*. Baltimore: John Hopkins University Press.

Littlewood. R. and Lipsedge, M. (1989) *Aliens and Alienists: Ethnic Minorities and Psychiatry*. London: Unwin Hyman.

Mace, C. (ed.) (1995) *The Art and Science of Assessment in Psychotherapy*. London: Routledge.

McCormick, E. (1994) Cognitive analytic therapy in private practice, in A. Ryle (ed.), *Cognitive Analytic Therapy: Active Participation in Change*. London: John Wiley.

Mcleod, J. (1994) *Doing Counselling Research*. London: Sage.

Malan, D. (1963) *A Study of Brief Psychotherapy*. London: Plenum.

Malan, D. (1976) *The Frontier of Brief Psychotherapy*. New York: Plenum.

Malan, D. (1995) *Individual Psychotherapy and the Science of Psychodynamics*, 2nd edn. Oxford: Butterworth Heinemann.

Malan, D. and Osimo, F. (1992) *Psychodynamics, Training and Outcome in Brief Psychotherapy*, 2nd edn. Oxford: Butterworth Heinemann.

Mann, J. (1973) *Time-Limited Psychotherapy*. Cambridge, MA: Harvard University Press.

Mann, J. and Goldman, R. (1994) *A Casebook in Time-Limited Psychotherapy*. London: James Aronson.

Mathers, N., Shipton, G. and Shapiro, D. (1993) The impact of short-term counselling on general health questionnaire scores, *British Journal of Counselling and Guidance*, 21 (3): 310–18.

Mearns, D. and Thorne, B. (1988) *Person-Centred Counselling in Action*. London: Sage.

Mellor-Clark, J. and Shapiro, D. (1995) *It's Not What You Do – It's the Way That You Do It: The Inception of an Evaluative Research Culture in Relate Marriage Guidance*. Leeds: Psychological Therapies Research Centre.

Mollon, P. (1997) Supervision: a space for thinking, in G. Shipton (ed.), *The Supervision of Psychotherapy and Counselling: Making a Place to Think*. Milton Keynes: Open University Press. pp. 24–34.

Molnos, A. (1995) *A Question of Time: Essentials of Brief Dynamic Therapy*. London: Karnac.

Noonan, E. (1983) *Counselling Young People*. London: Methuen.

Oldfield, S. (1983) *The Counselling Relationship*. London: Routledge and Kegan Paul.

Parkes, C.M. (1980) Bereavement counselling: does it work?, *British Medical Journal*, 281: 3–6.

Parkes, C.M. (1985) Bereavement, *British Journal of Psychiatry*, 146: 11–17.

Parry, G. (1996) *NHS Psychotherapy Services in England. Survey of Strategic Policy*. Wetherby: Department of Health.

Parsons, M. (1982) Imposed termination of psychotherapy and its relation to death and mourning, *British Journal of Medical Psychology*, 55: 35–40.

Pearmain, R. (1996) Overview of training programmes, *Universities Psychotherapy Association Review*, 5: 9–12.

Phippen, M. (1994) The 1992/93 ASC survey of counselling services in further and higher education, *Association For Student Counselling Newsletter*, May: 4–10.

Potter, V. (1997) *Is Counselling Training for You?* London: Sheldon Press.

Rogers, C. (1951) *Client-Centred Therapy*. Boston: Houghton Mifflin.

Rogers, C. (1967) *On Becoming a Person*. London: Constable.

Rogers, C. (1990a) A theory of therapy, personality and interpersonal relationships, as developed in the client-centred framework, in H. Kirschenbaum and V.L. Henderson (eds), *The Carl Rogers Reader*. London: Constable.

Rogers, C. (1990b) A client-centred/person-centred approach to therapy, in H. Kirschenbaum and V.L. Henderson (eds), *The Carl Rogers Reader*. London: Constable.

Roth, A. and Fonagy, P. (1996) *What Works for Whom?* New York: Guilford.

Rosenfeld, H. (1965) *Psychotic States*. London: Hogarth Press.

Rowan, J. (1993) Counselling for a brief period, in W. Dryden (ed.), *Questions and Answers in Counselling*. London: Sage. pp. 28–31.

Rowan, J. (1995) Private communication.

Royal College of Psychiatrists and British Psychological Society Council Report 37 (1995) *Psychological Therapies for Adults in the NHS*. London.

Ryle, A. (1990) *Cognitive Analytic Therapy: Active Participation in Change*. Chichester: John Wiley.

Ryle, A., Spencer, J. and Yawetz, C. (1994) When less is more or at least enough. Two case examples of 16 session cognitive analytic therapy, *British Journal of Psychotherapy*, 8 (4): 401–12.

Sayee Kumar (1996) Personal communication.

Segal, B. (1993) Attachment and psychotic processes in an anorexic adolescent, *Journal of Child Psychotherapy*, 19 (2): 53–67.

Seligman, M. (1996) The effectiveness of psychotherapy, *American Psychologist*, 50 (12): 965–74.

Shamni, S. (1985) *Bulletin of BAP*, July: 41–55.

Shapiro, D. and Barkham, M. (1993) *Relate – Information Needs Research*. Rugby: Relate.

Shea, M.T., Pilkonis, P.A., Beckham, E., Collins, J.F., Elkin, I., Scotsky, S.M. and Docherty, J.P. (1990) Personality disorders and treatment outcome in the NIMH treatment of depression collaborative research program, *American Journal of Psychiatry*, 147 (6): 711–18.

Shipton, G. (1994) Swords into ploughshares: working with resistance to research, *Counselling*, 5 (1): 38–40.

Shipton, G. (1996) *Counselling, the BAC Reader*. London: Sage.

Shipton, G. (ed.) (1997) *The Supervision of Psychotherapy and Counselling*. Milton Keynes: Open University Press.

Shipton, G. and Smith, E. (eds) (1993) *Perspectives on Evaluation and Research in Counselling*. ASC occasional paper. Rugby: Association for Student Counselling.

Sinason, V. (1997) What price trust? The struggle against personal corruption in straitened circumstances, in E. Smith (ed.), *Integrity and Change: Mental Health in the Market Place*. London: Routledge.

Smith, E. (1997) Private selves and shared meanings or forgive us our projections as we forgive those who project into us, *Psychodynamic Counselling*, 3 (2): 117–31.

Spearman, P. (in progress) *Effectiveness and Safety in Counselling*.

Stiles, W.B., Shapiro, D. and Elliot, R.K. (1986) Are all psychotherapies equivalent?, *American Psychologist*, 41: 165–80.

Storr, A. (1979) *The Art of Psychotherapy*. London: Secker and Warburg, and Heinemann.

Syme, G. (1994) *Counselling in Independent Practice*. Buckingham: Open University Press.

Talmon, S. (1990) *Single Session Therapy: Maximising the Effect of the First (and often only) Therapeutic Encounter*. San Francisco: Jossey-Bass.

Tantam, D. (1995) Why assess?, in C. Mace (ed.), *The Art and Science of Assessment in Psychotherapy*. London: Routledge.

Thorne, B. (1992) Psychotherapy and counselling: the quest for difference, *Counselling*, 3 (4): 244–8.

Thorne, B. (1996) Person-centred therapy, in W. Dryden (ed.), *Handbook of Individual Therapy*. London: Sage. pp. 121–45.

Tolley, K. and Rowland, N. (1995) *Evaluating the Cost-Effectiveness of Counselling and Health Care*. London: Routledge.

Trayner, B. and Clarkson, P. (1992) What happens if a psychotherapist dies, *Counselling*, 3 (1): 23–4.

Walker, M. (1992) *Surviving Secrets*. Buckingham: Open University Press.

Wangh, M. (1979) Some psychoanlytic observations on boredom, *International Journal of Psycho-Analysis*, 60: 515–27.

Ward, J. (1996) E-mail discussion, Psych-Couns.

Watkins, C.E. and Schneider, L.J. (1991) *Research in Counselling*. Hillsdale, NJ: Lawrence Erlbaum.

WHO (1992) *The ICD-10 Classification of Mental and Behavioural Disorders. Clinical Descriptions and Diagnostic Guidelines*. Geneva: World Health Organisation.

Wilkins, P. (1997) *Personal and Professional Development for Counsellors*. London: Sage.

Wilson, P. (1997) A time to think, in E. Smith (ed.), *Integrity and Change: Mental Health in the Marketplace*. London: Routledge.

Winnicott, D.W. (1958) *Collected Papers: Through Paediatrics to Psychoanalysis*. London: Tavistock.

Worden, J.W. (1983) *Grief Counselling and Grief Therapy: A Handbook for the Mental Health Practitioner*. London: Tavistock/Routledge.

Yariv, G. (1995) Crossing the threshold, *British Journal of Psychotherapy*, 11 (4): 506–13.

Index